Four Square (4□)

The Total Writing Classroom

for Grades 5-9

Written by Judith S. Gould and Evan Jay Gould

Illustrated by Ron Wheeler

Teaching & Learning Company

1204 Buchanan St., P.O. Box 10
Carthage, IL 62321-0010

This book belongs to

_____

Cover photos by Images and More Photography

Pictures © Corel Corporation

Copyright © 2002, Teaching & Learning Company

ISBN No. 1-57310-334-9

Printing No. 9876543

Teaching & Learning Company
1204 Buchanan St., P.O. Box 10
Carthage, IL 62321-0010

Table of Contents

Dear Teacher or Parent,

This book is a resource for educators of students at all ages and all levels. The activities have been tried and tested in elementary and secondary classrooms including students with disabilities, second language learners and students of different learning modalities. While the projects and activities are tailor-made to work with the *Four Square Writing Method* books, they can be used to round out any program of writing instruction.

The first section of this book contains an overview and discussion of writing as it relates to the language arts. Exploring and taking advantage of the ways that all language learning is connected can help students use what they already know to learn new things.

Section two is designed to provide ideas for the big picture. It includes an overview of a total writing classroom, as well as management tools for writing projects.

The third section has a collection of activities that can be used as mini lessons, warm-ups or whole class instruction. These activities are geared to target the most troublesome of student writing habits.

Section four's exercises can be used as an addendum and accompaniment to the *Four Square Writing Method*. They are geared to improving composition writing. While direct reference is made to the Four Square organizer, the lessons transfer easily to any organizational tool in use.

We hope you will use this book as a reference to provide a variety of exercises, activities and instruction and to make your writing classroom a fun and enriched environment.

Sincerely,

Judith & Evan

Judith S. and Evan Jay Gould

Section 1
The Language Arts

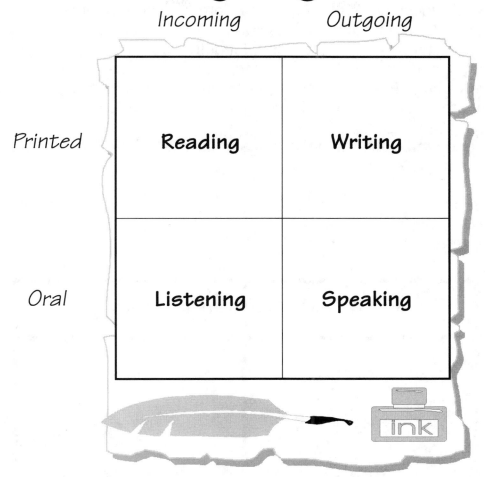

The four language arts do not exist in isolation. They are on a continuum. First, there are the two language arts that concern themselves with getting a message and decoding it. They are the incoming language arts, speaking and reading. Then, there are the two language arts that concern themselves with transmitting a message that others can interpret. They are the outgoing language arts, speaking and writing. Why include this basic information? Herein lies the answer to some key questions.

Why do so many kids have trouble with the idea of writing? Think about the family structure. In today's busy world, family time is shrinking. When we are scurrying about, there is less time for discussion. Less discussion means that kids have less opportunity to produce outgoing language (in the oral form). Also, think about the increased class sizes and packed standards manuals. In the classroom we have less and less time for kids to develop ideas in spoken discourse.

How can this information help? Tell parents to **talk** with their children. Talk about a specific topic. Retell the events of a day. Explain why they liked or disliked a particular event or occasion. Structuring language for an oral outgoing message requires similar thought processes to the writing exercise. When you share a story, movie or television program, discuss it. This is the most natural way to reinforce the comprehension skills that are a part of the reading program.

What about classroom applications? Sometimes kids need to see the big picture. Show students the way that the language arts fit together. This may be all that reluctant writers need. We need to remove the aura of mystery from the act of writing. Showing kids that "talking on paper" is all that writing really is can remove the barriers for many kids. As educators it is also important for us to understand that the four language arts affect one another. The writing that students do effects the reading they will choose. Language they hear comes out in the writing. Effective instruction in the language arts takes place when one form supports another. So many of our young students learn to read because they write.

Understanding and employing the basic ideas of language learning is important for all teachers and parents, too.

As we . . .	It helps us to . . .
Listen	Speak
Speak	Write
Write	Read
Read	Listen
Write	Speak
Listen	Write
Read	Speak

Dear Parent,

As your child's teacher I am concerned with all of his or her language learning. Together we can help your child become a successful reader and writer. You have already provided your child with many language lessons yourself. Because all language learning is related, I want to remind you of the importance of language in the everyday life of your child.

By listening to you, your child learned about producing oral language. To help your child learn to read and write, continued listening is needed. We are models for the language that children will produce. If we want our children to become efficient writers, it is important that we also help them become efficient speakers. Research has proven that practice in oral language helps build the skills in written language.

I have included some strategies that you can apply at home that will help build your child's communication and comprehension skills. Please don't hesitate to ask me any questions you may have regarding these strategies.

Sincerely,

Your Child's Teacher

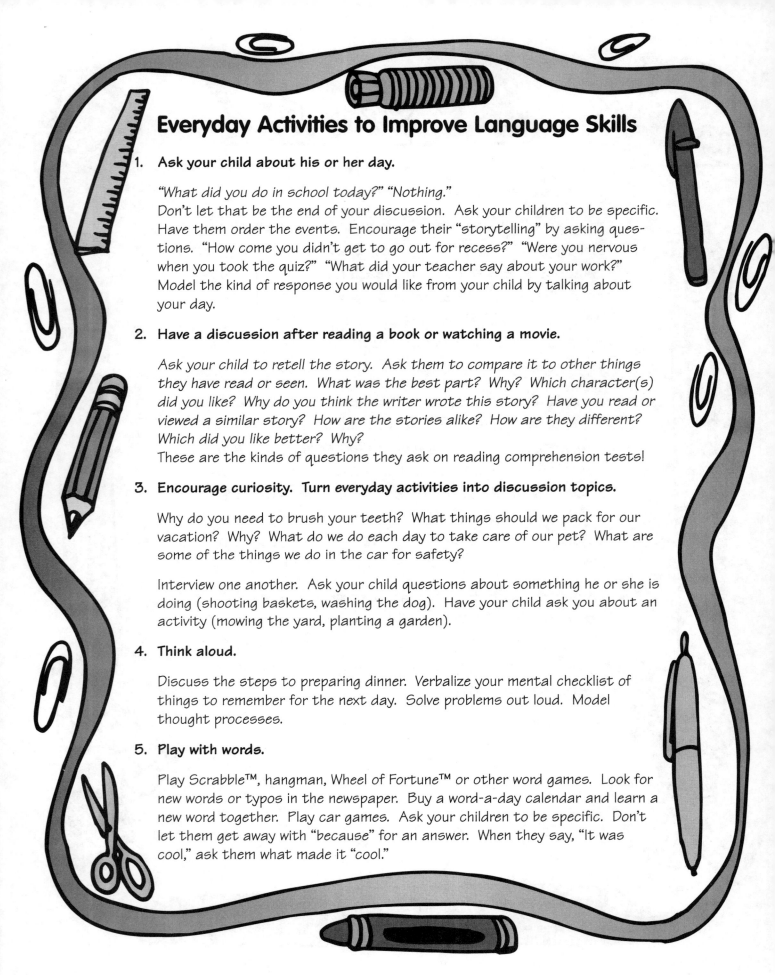

Everyday Activities to Improve Language Skills

1. **Ask your child about his or her day.**

   "What did you do in school today?" "Nothing."
   Don't let that be the end of your discussion. Ask your children to be specific. Have them order the events. Encourage their "storytelling" by asking questions. "How come you didn't get to go out for recess?" "Were you nervous when you took the quiz?" "What did your teacher say about your work?" Model the kind of response you would like from your child by talking about your day.

2. **Have a discussion after reading a book or watching a movie.**

   Ask your child to retell the story. Ask them to compare it to other things they have read or seen. What was the best part? Why? Which character(s) did you like? Why do you think the writer wrote this story? Have you read or viewed a similar story? How are the stories alike? How are they different? Which did you like better? Why?
   These are the kinds of questions they ask on reading comprehension tests!

3. **Encourage curiosity. Turn everyday activities into discussion topics.**

   Why do you need to brush your teeth? What things should we pack for our vacation? Why? What do we do each day to take care of our pet? What are some of the things we do in the car for safety?

   Interview one another. Ask your child questions about something he or she is doing (shooting baskets, washing the dog). Have your child ask you about an activity (mowing the yard, planting a garden).

4. **Think aloud.**

   Discuss the steps to preparing dinner. Verbalize your mental checklist of things to remember for the next day. Solve problems out loud. Model thought processes.

5. **Play with words.**

   Play Scrabble™, hangman, Wheel of Fortune™ or other word games. Look for new words or typos in the newspaper. Buy a word-a-day calendar and learn a new word together. Play car games. Ask your children to be specific. Don't let them get away with "because" for an answer. When they say, "It was cool," ask them what made it "cool."

The Two Voices of Writing

Writing teachers have the daunting task of fostering creativity while also teaching basic skills. This is because there are two voices in writing. One voice is nurtured with activities like field trips, cooking, exploring nature and other in-school experiences. The other voice is developed, among other things, such as the disciplines of grammar, spelling and punctuation.

Both voices need to be addressed in a complete language arts program. In fact, even programs that lean heavily on the creative process ("if you experience it, you can write about it" programs) need to include some structure. Imagine teaching a third grader multiplication by only using manipulatives. Yes, the youngster will have a lot of fun sorting candy, dry cereal, peanuts, etc. . . ., but eventually, you must introduce the times tables. If you don't, you're not being very fair to the student.

The Creative Voice
The "Warm and Fuzzy" Voice
Creativity
Sense of Story
A Writer's Ear
Life Experiences
Appreciation of Word Power
Variety of Experiences with Literature
Humor
Wit
(Etc.)

The Disciplined Voice
The "Red Pen" Voice
Structure
Planning Skills
Thinking Skills
Organizational Skills
Vocabulary
Grammar
Spelling
Punctuation
Paragraphing
Transitional Devices
Sentence Structure
(Etc.)

Building Blocks

When we teach children to read, we use building blocks. These learning tools are taught in a sequential and organized manner. While much experience is gained from practicing reading, there are certain skills that must be directly taught before children are independent readers. They include, but are not limited to:

- Letter Recognition
- Consonant Sounds
- Long Vowels
- Short Vowels
- Phonemic Awareness
- Phonics
- Blends
- Diagraphs
- Sight Words
- Decoding Skills
- Context Clues
- Inference

When we teach children to write, we need similar building blocks. These tools form the child's "bag of tricks" to be used again and again throughout his or her life. Without them, even the most creative students will find it hard to be understood. Writing, after all, is a form of communication. These building blocks include, but are not limited to:

- Structure
- Planning Skills
- Organization
- Grammar
- Vocabulary
- Spelling
- Sentence Structure
- Paragraphing
- Punctuation
- Transitions
- Elaboration

Teaching Those Skills

When teaching reading, there are many programs and organizational techniques to help you with the building blocks. Some teachers vow that reading groups are the best way to teach reading, while others prefer direct instruction. Some schools buy into programs like Accelerated Reader or SRA. Students in methods and practices courses debate over how much phonics and how much whole language should comprise a reading program. Even consumer products have joined the bandwagon. Who hasn't seen a commercial for "Hooked on Phonics" or other reading games or tutorials? All of this makes the case that reading is a subject that can be mastered with instruction.

O.K., how about writing? There isn't a pre-packaged "Hooked on Writing," not yet anyway. Most teachers, however, are familiar with the two popular components to writing instruction; Journals and The Writing Process. But these are only two components of a complete writing program.

Section 2
Activities for Your Writing Classroom

The Writing Classroom

You are bombarded by national, state, local and even school-based standards and expectations. You carefully prepare students for writing assessments because they carry high stakes for your school, district and sometimes for your own career. Students read and write, and they also write across the curriculum. So what else is needed in your writing classroom?

1. Wordplay

Some of the elements that need to be included in the complete writing program can fill a void in the way children play. As kids, many of us played word games. Crossword puzzles, Scrabble™, Mad Libs™ and even hangman occupied idle or rainy days. Today, kids have their own TVs, snappy electronic devices and even the internet to occupy their time. They are missing out on a wonderful opportunity to learn words, patterns, spellings and contexts. Kids today just don't play with words, so wordplay is a component of the total writing classroom.

2. Writing Process Projects

Writing is a form of art, work and communication. To reinforce these purposes, students should engage in a variety of writing projects. These projects can be navigated using the writing process. It is hard work to get from idea to presentation and all the steps in between. Longer projects using various processes are great opportunities to learn and grow.

3. Writing Conferences

Whether teacher/student or student/student, conferences provide the kind of invaluable one-on-one feedback that authors want and need in order to hone their skills. Managing conferences, keeping them informative and objective, is no small task, but a good conference often results in a depth of understanding that yields good writing.

4. Readers' Responses

Writing should be tied closely to its sister language art, reading. Journaling or prepared responses to literature, poetry and even non-fiction are great places to stretch learning across the curriculum.

5. Freeform Journals

Writing communicates and sometimes helps us work out the ideas and feelings we have, so free-form journaling based on our own experiences is an important practice.

6. Specific Instruction

Mini-lessons designed to target areas of need are most effective. Taken as a part of a writing process project, specific skills can be worked out for a meaningful purpose. Grammar, spelling and mechanics have the most meaning taught in context of the writing. Writing to a demand-prompt or assessment is also a skill that can be taught. The Four Square Method can be a component of this specific instruction.

The Writing Process

Most literature on the instruction of writing is based on using the writing process. The writing process is a multi step procedure that a writer completes when going from original idea to completed and published work. This process has a prescribed sequence of steps which vary in number and name. Some common terminology for the writing process steps follow.

Focusing	Topic choice, brainstorming
Ordering	Organizing the storm
Drafting	Getting it on paper
Revising	Editing—making the writing better
Proofreading	Correcting the mistakes
Publishing	Sharing it with others

Through the writing process many skills can be taught and reinforced. With proper planning, focused mini-lessons can guide writers. The most valuable writing instruction, the small-group or individual writing conference, usually takes place as a part of the writing process.

Planning meaningful projects for writers is a key to having a successful unit. Try using the planning page (see page 16) as you plan an activity. It can help to focus on the end result. It is important to remember that not every writing activity needs to assess and practice every skill. The scoring rubric for assessing students' work also flows naturally from this plan sheet. Once the unit is planned, the greatest challenge is to provide experiential and prewriting activities that can motivate writers to develop an interest in the project.

Not every project will follow this plan, but if you have the qualities of writing in mind, and you have the rubric that you will use to score the completed project, all you have left to do is the hard part, teaching!

To begin a project, some type of motivator is appropriate. Whether the prompt for writing comes from literature, a field trip, a classroom visitor or a student's bloody nose, the benefits of a real experience cannot be underestimated in writing. It is also important to have many good writing models around. Try to let the students see you writing, especially early on in the year. Showing them that writing is important beats telling them. Also let them know that writing is hard, but rewarding, work. Let them see you struggle, and let them see you celebrate.

When the writing process is complete, please let students publish. Use an author's chair or a reader's tea. An author's chair can be fun to include in your literacy center. It can be a plastic lawn chair, decorated in any way imaginable. Write on it with a permanent marker, or splatter it with colorful paint. Make it special. When an author sits in the chair to read, everyone listens and respects the amount of work it took to get to that chair. Have students applaud or snap their fingers (coffeehouse style) in support of one another.

Planning for the Writing Process Project

Challenge: What is the topic of the activity?

_____

Form: What style of writing will this be?

Expository   Persuasive   Narrative   Descriptive

Comparative   Poetry   Response   Other: _____

Function: What is the writer's purpose and audience?

Purpose: _____

Audience: _____

Style: What writing style should be used?

Figurative language: _____ 1st, 2nd or 3rd person

Passive or active voice   Formal or informal

Organization: How will the project be arranged?

Chronologically   Spatially   Most to least important   Least to most important

Business letter   Note   Comparison by attribute   Comparison by point

Other: _____

Mechanics: What mechanical skills do I expect my writers to exhibit as mastery?

Spelling   Ending   Punctuation   Capitalization   Quotations

Commas   Hyphens   Semicolons

Mini-Lessons: What specific writing skills will I teach in conjunction with this unit?

Hooks   Transitions   Endings   Elaboration   Effective dialogue

Others: _____

Scoring Rubric for the Writing Process

	Definitely	Mostly	Not Enough

Challenge: The writing addresses the topic.   _____ _____ _____

Topic: _____

Form: This writing is in the proper form.   _____ _____ _____

Form: _____

Function: The writing addresses the audience.   _____ _____ _____

Audience: _____

Style: The writing fits the style.   _____ _____ _____

Style(s): _____

Organization: The writing is organized properly.   _____ _____ _____

Organization: _____

Mechanics: Mechanical skills are mastered.   _____ _____ _____

Specific Mechanical Skills: _____

Mini-Lessons: Specific writing skills are used.   _____ _____ _____

Writing Skills: _____

Super Brownie Points: _____   **Total Score:** _____

Comments: _____

_____

17

Your Guide to the Writing Process

Getting a writing project from start to finish

Focusing	What can I write about? Do I have any ideas? Can I brainstorm with a buddy? Do I need help getting started?
Ordering	How can I put my ideas in order? Can I use a Four Square? Can I use another organizer? Do I have ideas for a beginning, middle and end?
Drafting	Write it down. Skip lines. Use pencil or erasable ink. Don't worry about the stuff you'll need to fix later.
Revising	Get someone to read it. Am I getting my message across? Did I grab my reader? Is the ending snappy? Did I choose strong words? Can I combine sentences? Do I need to get rid of any repeated information? Can I add some detail to clarify?
Proofreading	Check spelling. If unsure, ask a buddy. Paragraphs O.K.? Capitals and punctuation? Is my writing clear and neat? Is MY NAME on my final copy?
Publishing	Share. Brag. Gloat. Enjoy. You did it!

Sample Writing Project

Challenge: What is the topic of the activity?

Students will write a business letter. They will express an opinion or make a consumer complaint.

Form: What style of writing will this be?

Expository   (Persuasive)   Narrative   Descriptive

Comparative   Poetry   Response   Other: _____ *Business letter*

Function: What is the writer's purpose and audience?

Purpose: _____ *To change someone's mind, or to receive compensation.*

Audience: _____ *The school newspaper or business involved.*

Style: What writing style should be used?

Figurative language: _____   (1st) 2nd or 3rd person

Passive or active voice   (Formal) or informal

Organization: How will the project be arranged?

Chronologically   Spatially   Most to least important   (Least to most important)
Business letter   Note   Comparison by attribute   Comparison by point

Other: _____

Mechanics: What mechanical skills do I expect my writers to exhibit as mastery?

(Spelling)   (End punctuation)   Capitalization   Quotations
Commas   Hyphens   Semicolons   Punctuation

Mini-Lessons: What specific writing skills will I teach in conjunction with this unit?

Hooks   Transitions   (Endings)   Elaboration   Effective dialogue

Others: _____ *Writing persuasion in a respectful tone.*

Scoring Rubric for the Writing Process Sample

	Definitely	Mostly	Not Enough

Challenge: The writing addresses the topic. _____ _____ _____

    Topic: _Change someone's mind or make a consumer complaint._

Form: This writing is in the proper form. _____ _____ _____

    Form: _Persuasive/Business letter_

Function: The writing addresses the audience. _____ _____ _____

    Audience: _Business or newspaper_

Style: The writing fits the style. _____ _____ _____

    Style(s): _1st person_

Organization: The writing is organized properly. _____ _____ _____

    Organization: _Least to most important idea_

Mechanics: Mechanical skills are mastered. _____ _____ _____

    Specific Mechanical Skills: _Spelling, punctuation_

Mini-Lessons: Specific writing skills are used. _____ _____ _____

    Writing Skills: _Endings/Tone_

Super Brownie Points: _____   **Total Score:** _____

Comments: _____

_____

20

The Writing Conference

As with almost anything else, some of the most beneficial instruction for writers occurs in the most intimate setting. One-on-one conferencing is something that is daunting, even for the veteran to master, but it is worth the effort. In this setting, writers can work out the problems that they face on their individual pieces. A teacher or peer can address the specifics of the writing. Even with targeted mini-lessons for the whole class, some students are left out. In conferencing, nobody is left out.

The trick to the conference, of course, is how to entertain 29 or more students while working with only one! While there is certainly no easy answer to this question, there are certainly some management tips. Setting the ground rules for writing workshop and conference time will solve future conflicts.

Conferences can be done in different formats. Small groups work well with several writers at a "roundtable" discussion. You may need to facilitate these until they get the gist of the questioning. One on one can work well, but it is time consuming. Sometimes a whole class "conference" or evaluation can be done. Students can swap papers, and each reader or station can comment on a particular part of the paper. This engages the whole class (management) and saves time, too.

See swap conference reproducible on page 26.

Conferencing Rules

1. Students must come to the conference with something on the paper.

   Students shouldn't think that the conference is their opportunity to have you write them a paper! If you "give" too much in conference, then all the papers you read will sound just like you. Help them bring out their ideas, not reproduce yours.

2. Students may interrupt a conference only for a major emergency.

   Try the traffic light signal on the following page. Nobody can interrupt on red for anything but a major emergency. Yellow is for quick questions. Green indicates you are available.

3. The students should ask a buddy to read their work before the teacher conference.

   If it doesn't make sense to their buddy, it won't work for you either. You may want the students to have their buddies score the work on the project rubric, too.

See buddy conference reproducible on page 24.

Writing Conference Rules

1. Keep working silently during the conferences. Write, revise, proofread or read. If you confer with another, your voice must have a six-inch range.

2. Come to the conference with something on the paper.

   Don't think that the conference is an opportunity to have the teacher write your paper! Don't expect to "have" ideas given to you in conference. Conferencing will help you bring out your own ideas.

3. Interrupt a conference only for a major emergency.

   Nobody can interrupt on red for anything but a major emergency. Yellow is for quick questions. Green indicates that the teacher is available.

4. Ask a buddy to read your work before the teacher conference.

   If it doesn't make sense to your buddy, it won't work for the teacher, either.

Managing Writing Conferences

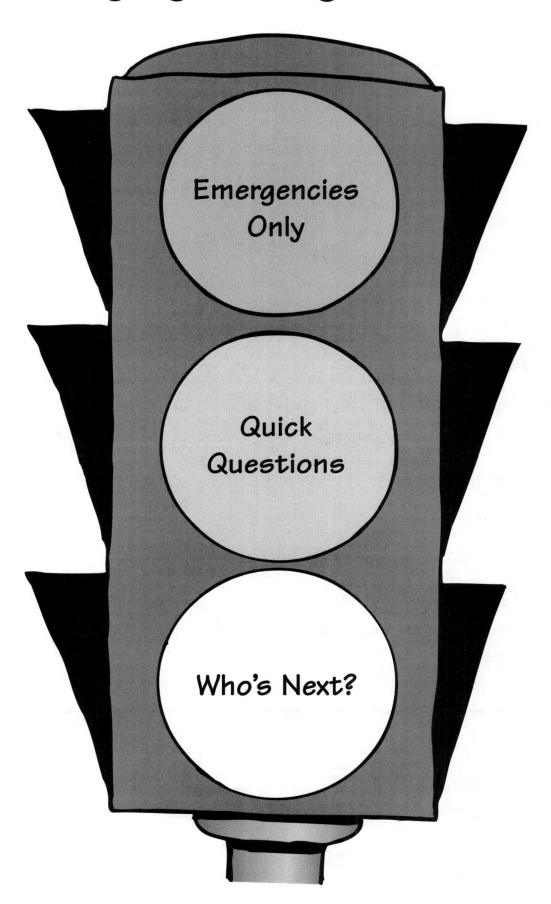

Buddy Conferences

Compliments

1. What is the best part of the writing? Why did you like it?

2. What interesting words did you like?

3. What good feeling did you get from the writing?

Questions

1. Is there a part that was confusing? Why?

2. Did the introduction catch your interest? Why or why not?

3. Did the ending make sense? Did it leave you hanging?

4. Is anything missing?

5. Is anything repeated?

6. If you could change one thing, what would it be?

7. Did you notice any problems in spelling, capitalization or punctuation? Can you tell your buddy where to get help for these?

TLC10334 Copyright © Teaching & Learning Company, Carthage, IL 62321-0010

Writing Conference Record

Date: _____ Class: _____ Piece: _____

Name: _____	Name: _____	Name: _____	Name: _____	Name: _____
Positive:	Positive:	Positive:	Positive:	Positive:
Negative:	Negative:	Negative:	Negative:	Negative:
Promise:	Promise:	Promise:	Promise:	Promise:
Name: _____	Name: _____	Name: _____	Name: _____	Name: _____
Positive:	Positive:	Positive:	Positive:	Positive:
Negative:	Negative:	Negative:	Negative:	Negative:
Promise:	Promise:	Promise:	Promise:	Promise:
Name: _____	Name: _____	Name: _____	Name: _____	Name: _____
Positive:	Positive:	Positive:	Positive:	Positive:
Negative:	Negative:	Negative:	Negative:	Negative:
Promise:	Promise:	Promise:	Promise:	Promise:
Name: _____	Name: _____	Name: _____	Name: _____	Name: _____
Positive:	Positive:	Positive:	Positive:	Positive:
Negative:	Negative:	Negative:	Negative:	Negative:
Promise:	Promise:	Promise:	Promise:	Promise:
Name: _____	Name: _____	Name: _____	Name: _____	Name: _____
Positive:	Positive:	Positive:	Positive:	Positive:
Negative:	Negative:	Negative:	Negative:	Negative:
Promise:	Promise:	Promise:	Promise:	Promise:
Name: _____	Name: _____	Name: _____	Name: _____	Name: _____
Positive:	Positive:	Positive:	Positive:	Positive:
Negative:	Negative:	Negative:	Negative:	Negative:
Promise:	Promise:	Promise:	Promise:	Promise:

Use this page to keep track of a whole class of conferences.

Swap Conference Sheet

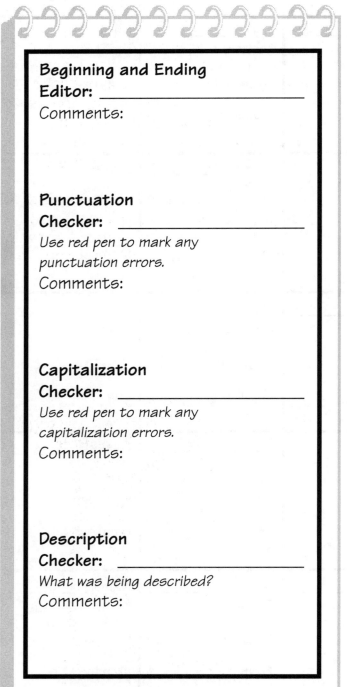

Beginning and Ending Editor: _____
Comments:

Punctuation Checker: _____
Use red pen to mark any punctuation errors.
Comments:

Capitalization Checker: _____
Use red pen to mark any capitalization errors.
Comments:

Description Checker: _____
What was being described?
Comments:

Beginning and Ending Editor: _____
Comments:

Punctuation Checker: _____
Use red pen to mark any punctuation errors.
Comments:

Capitalization Checker: _____
Use red pen to mark any capitalization errors.
Comments:

Description Checker: _____
What was being described?
Comments:

You can customize these "checkers" depending on the writing being worked on. You may have "rhyme checkers" for poetry or "form checkers" for a letter. You may also have spelling or fact checkers.

The Writer's Journal

Journal writing in the language arts is a routine exercise where writers respond to a prompted topic or write freely about the topic of their choice. Journals are not generally graded or corrected for grammar, punctuation, spelling or structural errors. A writer's journal is a storehouse of experiences and ideas that can be used to develop longer, more polished pieces of writing. Journals are a wonderful way to develop a writer's ear, sense of style, expression of voice and flow of language. Using journals, students open up and communicate. In the journal students can be wildly creative or deeply personal. Journaling helps to impart a very important purpose of writing, the expression of ideas and feelings. In journaling, this is a risk-free activity.

Journaling in the classroom can take on many forms. They are a great place to try out ideas. Sometimes students can write freely in their journals, and they will find that they have ideas for longer, more planned pieces of writing. The seeds started in the journal may be polished for future completed pieces. *See reproducible on page 28.*

The journal is also a great way to get to learn about your students. In the journal students may write freely about what is happening in their lives. Without the fear of correction or criticism that takes place in a finished piece of writing, the journal is a place where students write freely about their feelings.

Journals are well used as a place to respond to reading. A student may write about a particular book or story that he or she is reading. You may choose to post a poem to share with the class, and then ask them to journal a response. *See reproducible on page 29.*

In many classrooms, the journal is given a completion grade. That is, students are required to write a particular amount, say a page. In grading the journal, the teacher would only need to check for completion, and then perhaps journal back or comment on the student writing. In this way the paperwork is not overwhelming and the benefits of this activity can be enjoyed.

Journals, however, are not the best place for teaching those skills of discipline. If a red pen is taken to correct every error, students will not experiment with their language freely.

Free-Form Journal

Keep this list in your journal. Refer to it if you are not sure what to write about. Add to the list as you think of things you might like to explore in your writing.

1. What kind of day is it? What makes it this kind of day? How do you feel about the kind of day it is? What could you do to make it different? Should you do it? Why or why not? Will tomorrow be the same?

2. If you could live any where in the world, where would you live? Why? What century would you choose? Why? What is it like? Who are you? What do you do?

3. If you had $1,000,000 . . .

4. What is your favorite food? Color? Pet? Song? TV show? Movie? Actor? Book? Flavor? Season? Snack? etc.

5. What planet would you most like to visit? Why?

6. Tell about a time someone was really proud of you.

7. What is the best thing you can think of? Try answering this question as different characters from books you have read, or animals, or someone you know or make up. Explain your response.

Readers' Response Journal

Keep this list in your journal. Refer to it if you are not sure what to write about your reading.

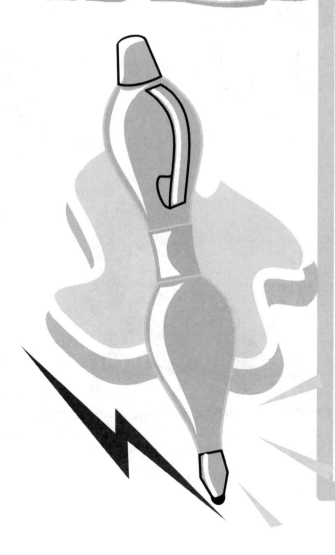

1. Retell the story or poem in your own words.
2. What did you notice in the story/poem?
3. What part of this did you like? Why?
4. What part did you dislike? Why?
5. Think of a way this story or poem relates to your own experience. Tell about it.
6. Does this story or poem remind you of any others you have read? Maybe a movie or TV show? Explain.
7. Did you notice any literary devices (simile, metaphor, personification, hyperbole, foreshadowing, symbolism, etc.)?
8. Why do you think the author wrote this?
9. Would you recommend this to a friend? Your teacher? Your mom? Why or why not?
10. Make suggestions about how the characters should solve their problems.

Section 3
Working with Words

Writing Warm-Ups That Work

Whether used for a class-starter or an ice breaker, these exercises do more than warm up the writer, they warm up the brain. They stimulate thinking "out of the box" and help rev up the creative juices.

No Repeat

The Objective: To improve word choice and sentence variety.

The Task: Students are to write 10 sentences on a particular prompted topic. (Younger students can write fewer sentences, or try this activity orally; it has the same benefits.)

The Catch: Once a word is used, it may not be repeated. If the word *is* has been used, it is finished. This applies to *the* and *and* as well. By the last few sentences, the words become really interesting.

Prompt: Ten sentences on the topic of family

1. My family is special.
2. We like to laugh together.
3. Grandpa always makes us giggle.
4. Grandma cooks delicious favorites.
5. Nat, a sister, works at Yankee Stadium.
6. Deb, the accountant, married Peter, computer specialist.
7. Mom resides in Miami and loves Chinese food.
8. Ilana, darling daughter of mine, dances ballet.
9. Evan, spouse, teaches music.
10. Reunions, though infrequent, are fun.

Name _____

Write 10 sentences on the topic listed below. Once you have used any word in a sentence, you may not repeat it.

Topic: Sports

1. _____
   _____

2. _____
   _____

3. _____
   _____

4. _____
   _____

5. _____
   _____

6. _____
   _____

7. _____
   _____

8. _____
   _____

9. _____
   _____

10. _____
    _____

Name _____

Write 10 sentences on the topic listed below. Once you
have used ANY word in a sentence, you may not repeat it.

Topic: Summer

1. _____
   _____

2. _____
   _____

3. _____
   _____

4. _____
   _____

5. _____
   _____

6. _____
   _____

7. _____
   _____

8. _____
   _____

9. _____
   _____

10. _____
    _____

Name _____

Write 10 sentences on the topic listed below. Once you have used any word in a sentence, you may not repeat it.

Topic: Going to the Movies

1. _____
   _____

2. _____
   _____

3. _____
   _____

4. _____
   _____

5. _____
   _____

6. _____
   _____

7. _____
   _____

8. _____
   _____

9. _____
   _____

10. _____
   _____

More Writing Warm-Ups That Work

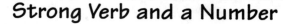

Strong Verb and a Number

The Objective: To introduce new vocabulary, and to encourage a variety of sentence structures.

The Task: Write an interesting or unusual action verb on the board. Define it and act it out, if necessary. Be sure that students understand the meaning of this new verb.

The Catch: Students are to write a sentence using this verb. The sentence must have a predetermined number of words. Ask for sentences on the high end, with 13 or more words. It may be amazing, but students do know how to include some detail!

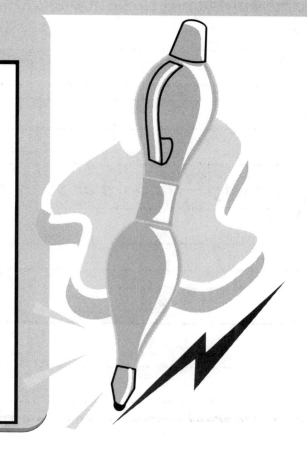

Strong verb, #: Aggravating 13

My little sister seems to enjoy aggravating me when I'm on the phone.

Strong verb, #: Interrogate 17

After her favorite lamp was broken, Mom had to interrogate everyone who was in the living room.

Name _____

Listed below are some "strong" verbs. Verbs are words that show an action. Using verbs like these helps our writing be strong, too. Use each verb in a sentence. Your sentence must have the number of words shown after the verb.

Verb: saunter—To walk at a leisurely pace, stroll.

11 Words

_____ _____ _____ _____ _____

_____ _____ _____ _____ _____ _____

Verb: berate—To scold for a long time.

9 Words

_____ _____ _____ _____

_____ _____ _____ _____ _____

Verb: sputter—To shout explosively in confusion.

12 Words

_____ _____ _____ _____ _____ _____

_____ _____ _____ _____ _____ _____

Verb: nudge—To poke or push gently.

14 Words

_____ _____ _____ _____ _____

_____ _____ _____ _____ _____

_____ _____ _____ _____

Name _____

Listed below are some "strong" verbs. Verbs are words that show an action. Using verbs like these helps our writing be strong, too. Use each verb in a sentence. Your sentence must have the number of words shown after the verb.

Verb: detonate—To set off in a burst of activity, to explode.
10 Words

_____ _____ _____ _____ _____

_____ _____ _____ _____ _____

Verb: evade—To slip away to hide.
8 Words

_____ _____ _____ _____

_____ _____ _____ _____

Verb: astound—To fill with bewilderment or wonder, to surprise.
13 Words

_____ _____ _____ _____ _____

_____ _____ _____ _____ _____

_____ _____ _____ _____ _____

Verb: trudge—To walk or march steadily and with effort.
12 Words

_____ _____ _____ _____ _____ _____

_____ _____ _____ _____ _____ _____

Noun Verbs

See reproducible page.

The Objective: To improve word choice.

The Task: Students are given a short list of nouns. They are to write several sentences (or a paragraph) using these words.

The Catch: Although these words are nouns, they must be used as verbs. For example, *rug* is a noun. But what if I rugged the floor?

Noun: Grass

Every year my neighbor has to grass his lawn all over again. You see, water is pretty expensive around here. Mr. Jones doesn't like to pay high water bills. So every summer he lets his lawn get crispy and dry out. It eventually dies. Sure enough the next year he is putting fresh sod down over the dead stuff. Doesn't he know that it would be cheaper to water? If you're in my neighborhood this spring, be sure to see Mr. Jones grass his lawn!

To many students of the English language, this noun-verb thing is getting out of hand. Many noun-verbs are so common we hardly give them a thought (perhaps you have telephoned someone today, or e-mailed them). Others are creeping into acceptance. (He authored another book.) To some this is how language evolves, and the creative force of enlisting a noun into service as a verb is where language stays fresh and alive. To others it is carelessness bordering on travesty and no way to treat the rules of grammar and civilized speech.

Name _____

The following words are usually nouns. Nouns are people, places or things. You are to change these nouns into actions. Using each noun as an action word, write a short story.

Nouns: pencil   paper   crayon   staple   marker

_____

_____

_____

_____

_____

_____

Nouns: shoe   sock   shirt   pants   jacket

_____

_____

_____

_____

_____

_____

Name _____

The following words are usually nouns. Nouns are people, places or things. You are to change these nouns into actions. Using each noun as an action word, write a short story.

Nouns: fork   spoon   knife   plate   dinner

_____

_____

_____

_____

_____

Nouns: dog   leash   sidewalk   neighbor   cat

_____

_____

_____

_____

_____

_____

No Fewer Than 9

The Objective: To improve sentence structure choice.

The Task: You may assign a topic or allow students freedom of topic choice. They are to write using exactly nine (or another number you designate) words per sentence.

The Catch: Wow, this forces students to think before they write.

Any sentence with more than nine words!

I have recently begun to learn how to ski.

No Adjectives

The Objective: To improve word choice and encourage figurative language.

The Task: Bring in an object (teddy bear, photo of current teen idol) and ask students to write several sentences describing it.

The Catch: Students may not use any adjectives in describing. (Observe the similes, the comparisons. They can be wonderful!)

I am the color of trees, and my eyes are the color of the sea. A T-shirt covers my tummy, and overalls cover my legs. Fur is all over my body. Extra hugging has worn it out. Your cat would tower over me. Inside I have stuffing to soften me. You may wish to hug me for security at night.

Write, Don't Speak or, Instant Messages Off-Line

Writing is communication, and for some students the realization that writing is just talking on the page is tough. This activity is fun and non-threatening. It encourages all students to participate.

As students are entering the room write on the board, *Writing Is Communication.* If students ask questions, write the answers on the board. After they start to get the idea, write the rules.

1. Only my chalk (or dry-erase marker) talks.
2. After you talk, pass the chalk.
3. You may not erase.
4. Always be kind.

Once you do this activity, students will beg to do it again and again. You may wish to set aside a small "graffiti board" in your classroom for students to leave written messages for one another. It is a great way for students to get comfortable with writing as communication.

See reproducible rules poster on page 44.

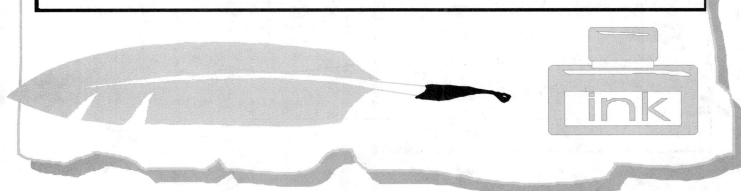

Instant Messages
Off-Line Rules

1. Only one person may talk at a time.
2. No slams or insults.
3. Teacher has the right to change the subject.
4. Chalk or marker must be passed to someone who has not had a turn before there are any repeats.
5. NO ERASING. Find space for your writing.
6. No other talking. The only talking is on the board.

The Unslam Book

Slam books usually have a negative connotation. However, using "unslam" books in your classroom can create a positive and rewarding activity.

Preparation: Each student needs several pieces of notebook paper and one 11" x 17" piece of construction paper.

Make the Book: The construction paper is folded in half with the notebook paper inside. Staple them together, and then use tape to cover the staples. The student may decorate the outside of the book. Make sure the student's name is large and on the front of the book.

The Writing: Each person begins with his or her own book. Set the timer for three minutes. In that time, direct students to write one or more sentences saying something nice about themselves. When the timer rings, everyone passes his or her book to the right. Set the timer again. This continues until everyone has had a chance to write something in everyone else's book. This is a great end-of-year activity and it makes a nice keepsake.

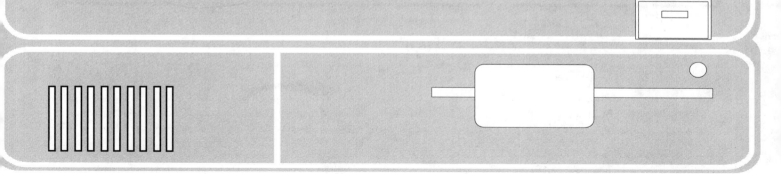

The Tattle Book

Tattling is a pet peeve for many teachers. Sometimes tattling is necessary, but most often the tattler is only seeking attention. How to cut down on the unnecessary tattling? Have them write it!

Preparation: Put together a binder with several copies of the "tattle page." (See reproducible on page 47.) Explain to students that any classroom event that does not involve bodily harm or danger is not an emergency. For these events you do not wish to be interrupted during teaching. Students can tattle by writing in the tattle book.

The Upkeep: Vow to check the tattle book and write a note back to the tattler. It really will save you the headaches of the constant "telling."

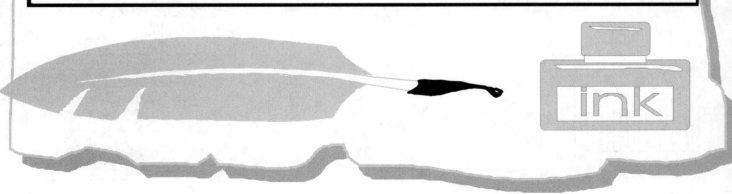

I'm telling.

Remember, anything dangerous
needs to be reported immediately.

My name: _____

Who did it: _____

What they did: _____
(What rule was broken)

When they did it: _____

Where they did it: _____

Who they did it to: _____

* * * * * * * * * * * * * * *

Teacher's comments: _____

_____

_____

Verbs Are Vivid

In good writing instruction, we certainly encourage students to be descriptive. Helping your readers "see the sights" is an important part of bringing them on the journey of your story. However, too often students think that description involves including a laundry list of adjectives before every noun. This is a sure way to kill reader interest.

Having the right word is more important than having the most words. And in many ways, verbs can be more descriptive than adjectives. Consider the following sentences:

The young, shiny, strong horse walked into the stable.
The horse pranced into the stable.

Or consider these:

The big, red, dented, rusted ship was in the harbor.
The ship rested in the harbor.

So, how can you encourage students to use more of these carefully chosen, descriptive verbs? One way is to bury the "dead" verbs. Page 51 is a poster that lists all the helping (dead) verbs. Early in the school year introduce these verbs to your students. Ask the students what verbs do. Invariably, they will tell you that they are the action words. Hand out "Act Out a Verb" cards to students. (See reproducible on page 49.) On some, write "dead" verbs. Write strong action verbs on the others. Then ask for student volunteers to "act out" the verbs in the style of a charades game. The others can try to guess the verbs. When the acting is done, the ones still holding cards can "bury" them.

Then, in remembrance of the "dearly departed" verbs, hand each student a sheet of those verbs to memorize. This is a great assistance in working with sentences. Also, once they know these "dead" verbs they can better avoid using them in their writing!

Act ouT a VerB	Act ouT a VerB	Act ouT a VerB	Act ouT a VerB	Act ouT a VerB
Act ouT a VerB	Act ouT a VerB	Act ouT a VerB	Act ouT a VerB	Act ouT a VerB
Act ouT a VerB	Act ouT a VerB	Act ouT a VerB	Act ouT a VerB	Act ouT a VerB
Act ouT a VerB	Act ouT a VerB	Act ouT a VerB	Act ouT a VerB	Act ouT a VerB
Act ouT a VerB	Act ouT a VerB	Act ouT a VerB	Act ouT a VerB	Act ouT a VerB
Act ouT a VerB	Act ouT a VerB	Act ouT a VerB	Act ouT a VerB	Act ouT a VerB

am	is	are	was	were
has	have	had	do	does
does	did	run	jump	dig
sing	hop	kick	point	kiss
be	being	been	could	should
stand	drink	hug	scratch	spin

Dead Verbs
(also known as helping verbs)

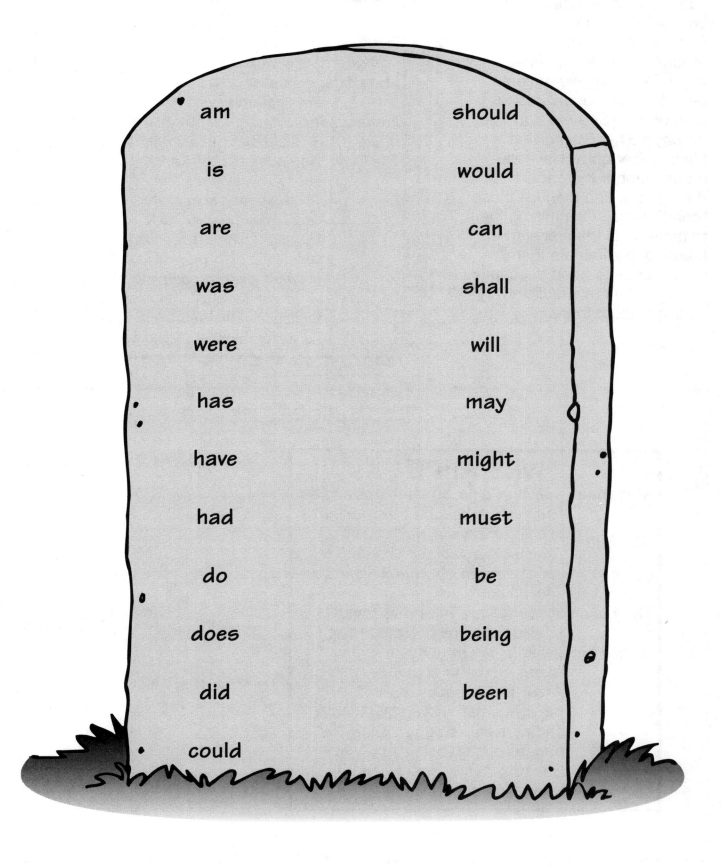

am	should
is	would
are	can
was	shall
were	will
has	may
have	might
had	must
do	be
does	being
did	been
could	

Activities with "Dead" Verbs

Here are some activities that you can do with your students to help them learn to work around these verbs. First, it is a good idea to give each student a list of these verbs to memorize. *(See reproducible on page 51.)* Then give a blank paper quiz. Have students number the page 1 through 23, and then list those "dead" verbs. Committing them to memory is the first step in learning to eliminate them. Then reinforce good descriptive writing habits by practicing writing without them.

Talk About

Invented by a student, this game practices oral description without "dead" verbs.

Materials: A poster or transparency projection of a picture.

Preparation: Divide students into two teams, lined up or seated in order.

The Play: As each student takes a turn, he or she is to say one, complete sentence about the picture. The sentence may contain no "dead" verbs. There is a three-second thinking time limit before speaking. If the student cannot complete the task, he or she is "out" and becomes the audience. The last team with a surviving member is the winner.

Who Am I?

Materials: Several objects that are similar such as a bunch of gardening tools or several dolls. Set them on a table in the center of the room where everyone can see them.

The Play: Students are given five minutes to describe one object on the table. They may not use any "dead" verbs in the description. After five minutes, collect all papers. Then move the objects on the table around. Pass the papers out to other students. See who can guess which object was being described.

Change That Word!

a game show for sentence improvement

You Need: a pocket chart on a stand is helpful
several sentence strips
two bells or buzzers
one host or hostess
one "Vanna"
two players
a judge and scorekeeper

Get Ready: Think of a word that is in a state of overuse by your student writers (*nice, cool, awesome . . .*). On the sentence strips write five sentences using that word (underline the word). Put a point value on the back of the sentence strip (100-500 points). Then make five sentences for additional words. *You could make it more challenging by using more than five!*

Set up the sentences on the pocket chart. On the left edge put the overused word, then the five sentences beside it with the number side up.

The Play: Decide who will go first. The player chooses a word. "Vanna" flips the sentence strip. The host reads the sentence. After the sentence is read, the first player to ring in gets a chance to CHANGE THAT WORD, and says the sentence using another word. The next player may not repeat a word that has been used already. Play continues until all the strips are used, or until time is up. The winner is the player who has changed the most words. In the event of a tie, a lightning round could take place in which players are given a word, and the one who comes up with the most alternative words is declared the winner.

Cool

100 That shirt is really <u>cool.</u>

200 My friend bought a <u>cool</u> CD yesterday.

300 That movie was <u>cool.</u>

400 My best friend is <u>cool.</u>

500 Do you want to see something <u>cool?</u>

54

Fun

100 I had <u>fun</u> at the amusement park.

200 Did you have <u>fun</u> at the party?

300 Skateboarding is so <u>fun</u>.

400 I love to have <u>fun</u>.

500 Summertime is great <u>fun</u>.

Bad

100 My dog is <u>bad.</u>

200 I have a <u>bad</u> headache.

300 That milk tastes <u>bad.</u>

400 Did you hear the <u>bad</u> news?

500 I thought that movie was <u>bad.</u>

nice

100 Mrs. Smith is a <u>nice</u> teacher.

200 I had a <u>nice</u> time on summer vacation.

300 I will do something <u>nice</u> for my mom.

400 She baked a really <u>nice</u> cake.

500 You should be <u>nice</u> to others.

Awesome

100 My mom is <u>awesome</u>.

200 Skating is an <u>awesome</u> sport.

300 I saw an <u>awesome</u> bike at the store.

400 I had an <u>awesome</u> time at the beach.

500 There was an <u>awesome</u> wave there.

Walk

100 I like to <u>walk</u> on the beach.

200 I usually <u>walk</u> to school.

300 My grandfather doesn't <u>walk</u> well.

400 You should see that baby <u>walk</u>.

500 My angry sister <u>walked</u> into the room.

Said Is Dead

Needed

Two coffee cans. Cut slots in plastic lids. Make "Said is dead" labels for the cans, one in pink for girls and one in blue for boys.

Copies of Marc Brown's *D.W. All Wet*, or another young children's story that uses the word *said* repeatedly.

Part 1

Read the story. Use the inflection indicated by the cues in the dialogue (pretty flat when the author repeats *said*).

Have students rewrite the story, finding alternatives for *said*. Ask them to practice reading with the proper inflection. How has it changed the story?

Part 2

Set up the competition. Show students the two cans. Set them up in an accessible place in the classroom. Challenge the boys to beat the girls (and vice-versa) in a competition to put more alternatives for *said* in their can. Let the competition run for a week or two. To really heat it up, let them know the running totals. When the competition ends, you have a wonderful display of alternative words that the students have discovered. Post them in your classroom for use by all!

Said Is Dead

Give Me MORE!
a game show for sentence improvement

You Need: a pocket chart on a stand is helpful
several sentence strips
two bells or buzzers
one host or hostess
one "Vanna"
two players
a judge and scorekeeper

Get Ready: There are four categories. Write them on short sentence strips and place them at the left side of the long pocket: Who? What? How? and What's It Like?

For the quiz questions write five sentences (point values 100 -500) for each category. In the Who category, write using an ambiguous pronoun. The category uses *that* or *it* in the sentences. The How category uses a nondescript verb. The What's It Like category uses a simple, ordinary noun. On the reverse of the quiz questions write the point values 100-500.

The Play: Decide who will go first. The player chooses a category. "Vanna" flips the sentence strip. The host reads the sentence. After the sentence is read, the first player to ring in gets a chance to GIVE ME MORE, and says the sentence changing or adding more information. The next player may not repeat a change that has been used already. Play continues until all the strips are used, or until time is up. The winner is the player who has the most points.

Who?

100 She is really nice to me.

200 Did you see them dance on the stage?

300 I've never met her.

400 They really don't skate very well.

500 He has a lot of friends.

What?

100 It tastes terrible.

200 My mother has them.

300 What did you do with it?

400 They belong in the trash.

500 Get rid of it!

How?

100 Grandmother danced.

200 My teacher speaks.

300 Uncle Henry eats.

400 My baby sister cries.

500 I sing.

What's It Like?

100 The car sped down the street.

200 A bird circled around me.

300 The animal was scary.

400 My sneakers were expensive.

500 The skaters were cool.

Shrink It!
a game show for sentence improvement

You Need: an overhead projector and transparencies
lap sized dry-erase boards and markers
two bells or buzzers
one host or hostess
one "Vanna"
two players
a judge and scorekeeper

Get Ready: In this game you will need to prepare several groups of short sentences in advance. These groups of sentences must have common elements. The object of the game is to help students realize that they can combine the ideas in short sentences to make more interesting ones.

Examples:
1. My cat sleeps a lot. He is 14 years old. I love him.
2. My sister is thin. She eats healthy foods.

Potential Answers:
1. I love my 14-year-old cat, even though he sleeps a lot.
2. Because she eats healthy foods, my sister is thin.

The Play: "Vanna" exposes the first group of sentences on the overhead projector. The host reads the sentences. After the sentences are read, the players use the lapboards and markers to rewrite the short sentences into one combined sentence. The first player to ring in gets a chance to SHRINK IT. Play continues until all the sentences are used, or until time is up. The winner is the player who has the most points.

Triangle Sentences

a fun and easy way to improve those predictable and jaded sentence structures

Building triangle sentences can be completed individually or in groups. Students are first given a noun. They build a longer and more detailed phrase based on this noun until it becomes a complete sentence.

This example uses *bus* as the noun.

Bus

Bus rides

Rickety bus rides

Rickety bus rides slowly

Rickety bus rides slowly down the road

The rickety bus rides slowly down the road.

If the grammatical terminology is too difficult, then ask these questions:

(Given noun)

Does what?

What kind?

How does it do it?

Where does it do it?

Make the sentence.

Now students have written a sentence with a lot of information in it (this is also a great lead-in to grammar instruction). The next challenge is to slide around some of the information to create new and interesting sentences.

Triangle Sentences

Thirteen different ways to start a sentence!

1. **Regular Order**
   The rickety bus rides slowly down the road.
2. **Question**
   Does the rickety bus ride slowly down the road?
3. **Exclamation**
   How slowly the rickety bus rides down the road!
4. **Adverb First**
   Slowly, the rickety bus rides down the road.
5. **Prepositional Phrase First**
   Down the road the rickety bus rides slowly.
6. **Verb Precedes Subject**
   Down the road rides the rickety bus slowly.
7. **Quotation**
   "The rickety bus rides down the road slowly," he said.
8. **Apposition**
   The rickety bus, filled with cheerleaders and football players from our school, rides slowly down the road.
9. **Adjective First**
   Tired, the rickety bus rides slowly down the road.
10. **Adjective Phrase**
    Recently in a wreck, the rickety bus rides slowly down the road.
11. **Present Participle**
    Knocking loudly, the rickety bus rides slowly down the road.
12. **Perfect Participle**
    Having ridden down the road slowly, the rickety bus rested.
13. **Verb Opener**
    Yelled the driver, "The rickety bus rides slowly down the road."

Triangle Sentences

a fun and easy way to improve those predictable and jaded sentence structures

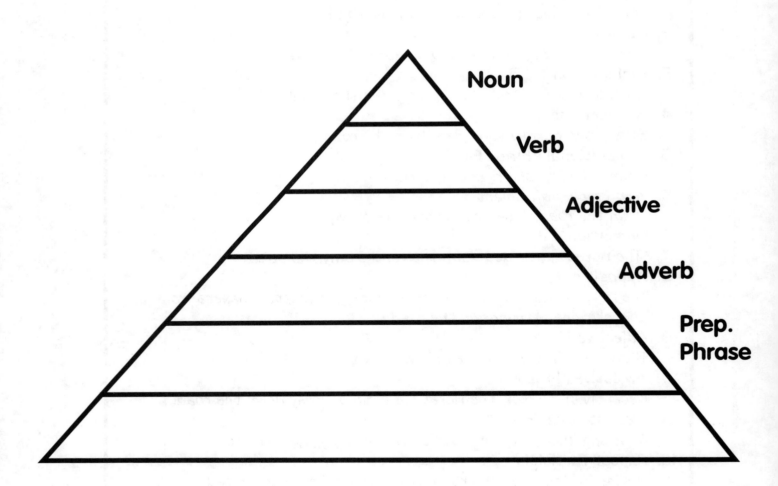

Noun

Verb

Adjective

Adverb

Prep.
Phrase

Homophone Help

Spelling instruction is an enigma for many. There are more exceptions than rules in our English language. As soon as a spelling pattern is learned, it is often forgotten. The same goes for those spelling lists. How often has a student tested correctly on a word only to spell it incorrectly in writing?

No quick fix for the spelling nightmare is offered here. But perhaps there is a way to eliminate some pet peeves.

How often are *there, they're* and *their* confused? How about *two, too* and *to*? These are words that our students know how to spell, but don't take the time to think about.

Create a pear tree in your classroom. That is a *pear pare pair* tree for your classroom! Use an indoor plant, design one on the wall, or make one out of cardboard carpet tubes (ask your local carpet store). As you encounter homophones in your reading and writing, students can take the *pare pear pairs* and add them to the tree. They will spell each word, and give an illustrated clue. Now good spelling is ripe for the picking!

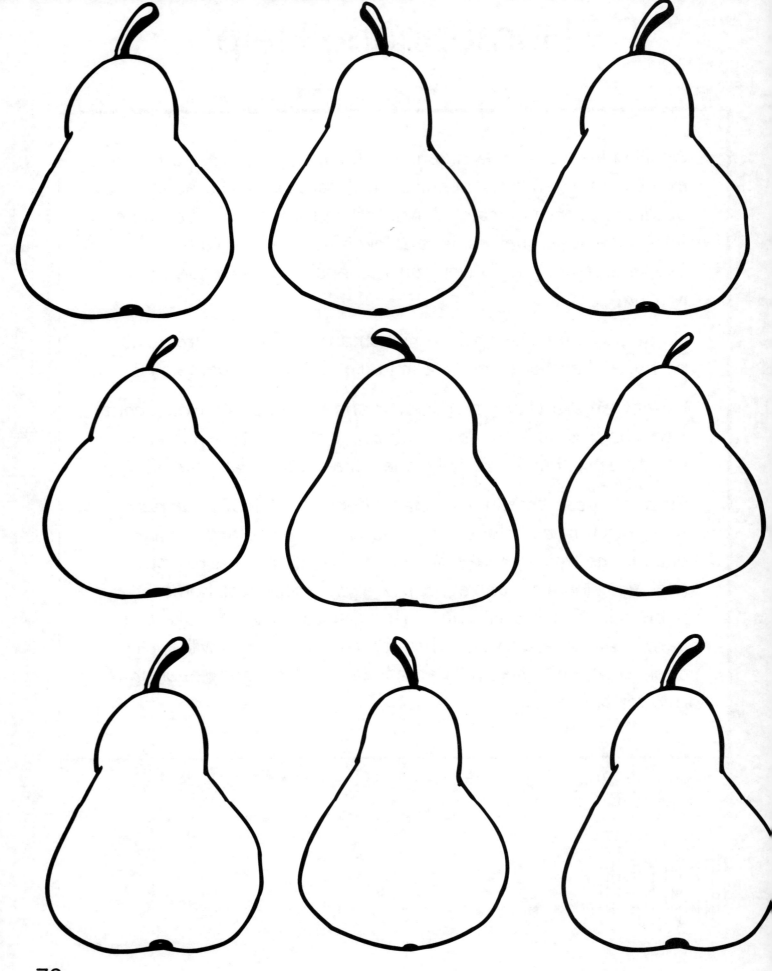

72

Adjectives

The "descriptive" part of speech. How is it that our students are able to reduce this multitude of omnipotent describers to *cool* and *awesome*? The following pages have a few, painless activities that can help your students explore the world of adjectives beyond *cool*.

The Adjective Acrostic Poem

These are great to do at the beginning of the year as a "getting-to-know-you" activity. For each letter of the child's name, he or she is to think of an adjective beginning with that letter. These acrostic poems make a nice accompaniment to a self-portrait drawing.

Joyful
Unselfish
Daring
Young

Mixing-Up Adjectives

What color is something sour? How about the taste of green? The sound of brown? Play with adjectives and mix the senses. Have students explore their own perceptions about their senses. A great addition to this activity is to write some poetry, using the "wrong" sense. Describe a forest based on the sounds, or your house based on the smells.

Lose the Adjectives

Yes, that's right. Sometimes the adjective is better replaced by the right noun.

Consider the following:

The little, clumsy, wobbly boy fell down.

The toddler fell down.

The Adjective Game

This game makes thesaurus use a fun challenge. Students will compete for the most adjectives to describe a picture.

Preparation: Find a few magazine pictures. Glue them to construction paper or tagboard. Divide students into teams of two or three. Each team should have a different color marker, a piece of paper and a thesaurus.

The Play: Each team starts with a different picture. Set a timer for three minutes. During this time, each team should try to list as many adjectives as possible to describe the picture writing them down with their colored marker. When time is up, the picture and the team's list is exchanged with another team. Now each team will add more adjectives to the list without repeating any found by the first team. Repeat this procedure for several rounds. The team with the most adjectives overall is the winner. Save the lists and pictures; they make wonderful bulletin board displays!

Spy Cam

This activity is a great warm-up, and it sometimes helps students who "have nothing to write" in their journals.

Students will write during the entire activity. They are to imagine that they are a security camera, or a spy camera. They can see and hear, and certainly record. In words, they are to record the actions in your classroom. A security camera would catch every sneeze, scratch and glance.

When the writing is done, have a few students share. Even the "shy" students volunteer for this activity. See who caught the most, and who missed things. It is amazing how much activity can take place in a room that is silent and filled with writers!

This is also a neat activity to do at the beginning of the year. In this case, students would be wearing name tags, so that the "cameras" can more easily record who is doing what.

Sometimes, during a writing workshop, it is a good idea to hire a secret spy cam. Having one student record the activities of everyone in the room can free you to complete individual or small group writing conferences. You can deal with any infractions later, thereby preserving precious writing time!

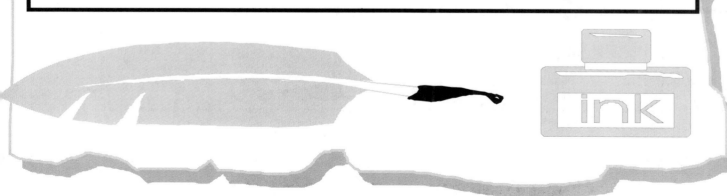

Show, Don't Tell

The best descriptive writing shows the reader what the writer sees; it doesn't tell. The "Show, Don't Tell" writing activity asks students to write a short piece describing a place, feeling or situation. The goal of this assignment is to provide the reader with specific and illustrative details about the five senses and the emotions of the characters without coming right out and stating the topic. This is best achieved by using a minimum of helping verbs (less than 10) and a generous dose of adjectives and adverbs. Compare the following examples of writing in response to the topic "I was hungry."

Example 1 (Incorrect): I was starving and I really wanted food. Everything looked good to me. I was so hungry. I couldn't wait to eat supper last night.

Example 2 (Better): I felt the grumbling come from deep within me. It started soft and then built to a roar. I walked by Fluffy's bowl, which was filled with foul-smelling fish, and even that tempted me. My imagination conjured images of juicy steak, potatoes and fresh salad. When would relief be served?

When the assignments have been collected, remove the authors' names and randomly number the papers. Pass the papers to the groups which will choose several papers as finalists. Read each finalist's paper aloud without disclosing the author's name. The class will then vote on the best "Show, Don't Tell." The winner can get a sweet treat or a certificate suitable for framing.

Some Suggested Topics

My room was messy.
The weather was beautiful.
I had a rotten day.
That teacher is mean.
I didn't feel well.
I enjoyed that roller coaster.
Dinner was delicious.
It's cold outside.
Thanksgiving was fun.
My picture came out horrible.
My vacation was great.

That party was awesome.
I think I'm in love.
I was frightened.
Those clothes were fine!
I was nervous.
That test was hard.
Spring break was wild.
What a lovely spring day.
I had a great day.
I was bored.
The weather is awful.

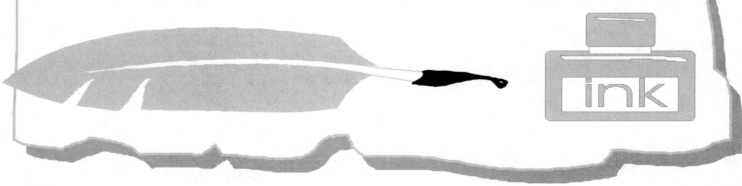

Show, Don't Tell Score Sheet

Scoring "Show, Don't Tell"

Paper #   Score   Reason

_____   _____   _____

_____   _____   _____

_____   _____   _____

_____   _____   _____

_____   _____   _____

_____   _____   _____

_____   _____   _____

Scoring "Show, Don't Tell"

Paper #   Score   Reason

_____   _____   _____

_____   _____   _____

_____   _____   _____

_____   _____   _____

_____   _____   _____

_____   _____   _____

_____   _____   _____

Scoring "Show, Don't Tell"

Paper #   Score   Reason

_____   _____   _____

_____   _____   _____

_____   _____   _____

_____   _____   _____

_____   _____   _____

_____   _____   _____

_____   _____   _____

Scoring "Show, Don't Tell"

Paper #   Score   Reason

_____   _____   _____

_____   _____   _____

_____   _____   _____

_____   _____   _____

_____   _____   _____

_____   _____   _____

_____   _____   _____

Show, Don't Tell

This certificate is presented to

_____

for excellent writing! Your classmates
chose your writing on the topic of

_____

as a Show, Don't Tell winner.

Congratulations!

_____ teacher

_____ date

Teaching the Use of Scoring Rubrics

A scoring rubric is a holistic device used to assess writing. That is, it takes into consideration the entire piece of writing. Usually, scoring rubrics identify certain attributes that are valued in a piece of writing. For instance, the organization, mechanics and use of detail may be scored. A rubric doesn't simply use a checklist, but assesses the overall merit of a piece.

Teaching the rubric is one way to help improve the success of your students. If they can understand how they will be scored, and what will be valued, then they may be able to include these things in their writing.

One activity that works well in rubric instruction is "Drawing to the Rubric." In this activity, students are given the prompt of a simple picture to draw. The picture is to be drawn to receive a certain score, based on a rubric. The students explain aloud why they think the picture would earn the score. In explanation, they must use the terminology on the rubric. This is a great way to learn more about how they will be scored, particularly on a high-stakes assessment. After students draw and present, post the rubric-scored pictures in the room, and list their attributes. These will serve as a reminder to students when they write.

Drawing to the Rubric

Sample Rubric

Focus	Organization	Supporting Detail
3 Focused on topic. Seems complete.	Logical progression. Clear organizational pattern.	Ample development. Elaboration of ideas.
2 Generally focused but may have some loosely related info.	Pattern evident but lapses may occur.	Some ideas lack detail to support or are illogical.
1 Minimally addresses the topic.	Little, if any pattern of organization.	Sparse support, or illogical detail.

Prompt: Draw a Cat

Score 3—Completed (whole cat) Organized in the correct order, lots of support (meow, whiskers, etc.).

Score 2—Generally focused (Some kind of animal), pattern of an animal, Illogical horns and tail.

Score 1—Minimally addresses topic (it is about an animal) random ideas and illogical detail.

The Cleaning Your Room Rubric

Rubrics can be developed for nearly any function. To develop a rubric, first think of what a nearly perfect situation would be. Then think of the things that you value. The rubric would have these things in the highest scoring category, and then slowly disintegrate to levels that are not up to par. Following is an example:

5

- Bed is made, no creases, pillows fluffed.
- Nothing is on the floor.
- All dresser drawers are closed.
- Surfaces of furniture are dust-free and clear.

4

- Bed is made, with only a few creases. The pillows are kind of fluffed.
- There are only small bits on the floor that the vacuum will surely pick up.
- Dresser drawers are closed, but one has something sticking out.
- Surfaces are cleared off, but there is some dust.

3

- Bed is made, and the pillows are on the bed.
- On the floor are only small bits for the vacuum and some of the clothes that wouldn't fit in the overstuffed drawers.
- Every drawer of the dresser has a piece of something sticking out of it.
- On the surfaces are some dust and maybe yesterday's snack.

2

- Bedclothes are on the bed.
- It will be possible to navigate the vacuum between the things on the floor.
- It seems impossible to close the dresser drawers.
- The surfaces of the furniture are visible.

1

- The bed is visible.
- It does look like some of the old food wrappers were picked up off the floor.
- Most of the things that belong in the dresser are near the dresser.
- I'm pretty sure there's furniture under there.

Unscorable or 0

- This room wasn't touched or, you mowed the lawn (or did something else) instead!

Section 4
Improving Compositions
Four Square and More

Three Levels of Support

Adding elaboration to writing is the highest level of support in writing. It makes the writing personal and adds vivid examples that "lend credibility" and support the topic. Young writers need lots of practice in recognizing and creating meaningful elaboration in their writing.

1. Explanation (Good)

2. Supporting Detail (Better)

3. Elaboration (Best)

To explain the three levels of support, let's imagine that our topic is to explain why it is fun to play baseball. The support would be developed like this:

It's fun to play baseball.

1. Explanation (Good)
Hitting the ball is awesome.

2. Supporting Detail (Better)
The best part is hitting a home run.

3. Elaboration (Best)
Once, it was the bottom of the 9th, there were two outs and we were down by one run. My pal Lucy Longlegs was on second. I saw my pitch and I went for it. That ball went over the fence and kept flying. We won and went on to become champions. Boy, do I love baseball!

A valuable exercise involves the use of student or model essays. Give the students three colors of hi-lighter markers. Explanation is colored green, supporting detail yellow and elaboration red. More red makes a better paper. Once they develop an eye and ear for elaboration, they will be more likely to include it in their own writing.

Find the three levels of support in the following essay. Color the explanation green, the supporting detail yellow and the elaboration red.

Weekends are great. They are a time to sleep in, play around and stay up late. I really love weekends.

One reason that weekends are great is that I usually sleep in. I can wear my comfy flannel pajamas longer. Sometimes I don't shower until the afternoon. My morning is for lounging around, instead of the usual weekday rush. Last weekend, for example, I slept until 11:00, had breakfast and then went back to sleep again! How relaxing!

Also, on weekends I get to play. I love to roller blade through the neighborhood on Saturdays. Sometimes, if it rains, we play board games like Monopoly™. One rainy weekend last year my sisters and I played a marathon game of Monopoly™ that lasted for 48 hours! I also like playing cards. Gin Rummy is a fun game to play on a lazy weekend.

Early to bed, early to rise . . . not on weekends! The most fun I have ever had on a weekend included staying up past midnight. I love watching late-night movies.

Snacking on popcorn and drinking a milk shake makes the experience complete. Once my two best friends slept over. We rented four movies and got lots of snacks. We didn't go to sleep until 3 a.m.!

So you see, weekends are a great time. I enjoy sleeping in, playing around and staying up late on weekends. I can't wait until Friday comes!

Answer Key

Some of these answers are subject to discussion, and discussion is good!

<u>Explanation</u>　　`Supporting Detail`　　**Elaboration**

Weekends are great. <u>They are a time to sleep in, play around and stay up late.</u> I really love weekends.

<u>One reason that weekends are great is that I usually sleep in.</u> `I can wear my` `comfy flannel pajamas longer. Sometimes I don't shower until the afternoon. My` `morning is for lounging around, instead of the usual weekday rush.` **Last weekend, for example, I slept until 11:00, had breakfast and then went back to sleep again! How relaxing!**

<u>Also, on weekends I get to play.</u> `I love to roller blade through the neighborhood on` `Saturdays. Sometimes, if it rains, we play board games like Monopoly™.` **One rainy weekend last year my sisters and I played a marathon game of Monopoly™ that lasted for 48 hours!** `I also like playing cards. Gin Rummy is a fun game to` `play on a lazy weekend.`

<u>Early to bed, early to rise . . . not on weekends! The most fun I have ever had on a</u> <u>weekend included staying up past midnight.</u> `I love watching late-night movies.` `Snacking on popcorn and drinking a milk` `shake makes the experience complete.` **Once my two best friends slept over. We rented four movies and got lots of snacks. We didn't go to sleep until 3 a.m.!**

So you see, weekends are a great time. I enjoy sleeping in, playing around and staying up late on weekends. I can't wait until Friday comes!

Find the three levels of support in the following essay. Color the explanation green, the supporting detail yellow and the elaboration red.

My favorite meal is spaghetti and meatballs. It's my favorite because it is easy, fun to eat and delicious. I could eat spaghetti and meatballs for dinner every night.

First, it's easy to make spaghetti and meatballs. You simply roll the meat into golf ball-sized pieces, then throw them in the pot. I use a huge, cauldron-sized pot. Pour on the store-bought sauce. My favorite brand is Mama someone or other. It is so easy to make, in fact, that I once prepared and served spaghetti and meatballs to 20 people. Dinner was ready in no time, and everybody loved it!

Also, my favorite meal is spaghetti and meatballs because it's fun to eat. I like to twirl it on my fork. It looks just like a twister. It's fun to slurp because it makes a loud smacking noise. I always splatter the sauce. When I'm done, it looks like an explosion. Last week we were eating spaghetti and meatballs when my meatball rolled off my plate and onto my sister's foot. Well, she got back at me by putting spaghetti in my hair. Soon our mom and dad joined in. We all laughed so hard! Spaghetti and meatballs is always a good time at my house.

Third, my favorite meal is spaghetti and meatballs because it's delicious. I like the tangy taste of red tomatoes. The Italian spices are great, especially the zippy garlic. The meat is very filling, like a hamburger. For as long as I can remember, spaghetti and meatballs has been the birthday dinner of my choice. We go to our favorite Italian restaurant, and I order the biggest plate they can carry.

So you can see, my favorite meal is spaghetti and meatballs because it's easy to make, fun to eat and delicious. Would you like to come over for some spaghetti and meatballs tonight?

Answer Key

Some of these answers are subject to discussion, and discussion is good!

<u>Explanation</u>　　Supporting Detail　　**Elaboration**

My favorite meal is spaghetti and meatballs. <u>It's my favorite because it is easy, fun to eat and delicious.</u> I could eat spaghetti and meatballs for dinner every night.

First, <u>it's easy to make spaghetti and meatballs.</u> You simply roll the meat into golf ball-sized pieces, then throw them in the pot. I use a huge, cauldron-sized pot. Pour on the store-bought sauce. My favorite brand is Mama someone or other. **It is so easy to make, in fact, that I once prepared and served spaghetti and meatballs to 20 people. Dinner was ready in no time, and everybody loved it!**

Also, <u>my favorite meal is spaghetti and meatballs because it's fun to eat.</u> I like to twirl it on my fork. It looks just like a twister. It's fun to slurp because it makes a loud smacking noise. I always splatter the sauce. When I'm done, it looks like an explosion. **Last week we were eating spaghetti and meatballs when my meatball rolled off my plate and onto my sister's foot. Well, she got back at me by putting spaghetti in my hair. Soon our mom and dad joined in. We all laughed so hard! Spaghetti and meatballs is always a good time at my house.**

Third, <u>my favorite meal is spaghetti and meatballs because it's delicious.</u> I like the tangy taste of red tomatoes. The Italian spices are great, especially the zippy garlic. The meat is very filling, like a hamburger. **For as long as I can remember, spaghetti and meatballs has been the birthday dinner of my choice. We go to our favorite Italian restaurant, and I order the biggest plate they can carry.**

So you can see, my favorite meal is spaghetti and meatballs because it's easy to make, fun to eat and delicious. Would you like to come over for some spaghetti and meatballs tonight?

Name _____

Find the three levels of support in the following essay. Color the explanation green, the supporting detail yellow, and the elaboration red.

Football has to be the best sport ever created. It has the greatest action and the coolest plays. Who could forget the cheerleaders? Football is awesome for many reasons.

The first thing I enjoy about football is the action. What other sport has running, tackling and such exciting throwing? During a football game you can't miss a minute, because the action is really non-stop. A lot can happen fast in a football game. Once at an NFL game I went to buy a hot dog, and I missed an interception and a touchdown!

Also, football has some interesting plays. The punt return is exciting because anything can happen when the ball is in the hands of the fastest player. Sometimes, a quarterback will sneak a running play and surprise the other team. The players all run in different patterns and fake out the defense. One time, during a playoff game of my favorite team, the game was won in the last seconds because of a sideways throw of the ball. We ended up scoring and got into the Superbowl!

Finally, I enjoy watching the cheerleaders. When my team isn't doing well, they cheer me up. Touchdowns bring a really fancy dance by these talented ladies. They really know how to get a crowd pumped. During the halftime show they usually do a dance to some of the most popular songs on the radio. Everyone in the stands dances along.

In conclusion, football is a great sport due to the action, plays and fabulous cheerleaders. What a great way to spend a Sunday afternoon.

88

Answer Key

Some of these answers are subject to discussion, and discussion is good!

<u>Explanation</u>   *Supporting Detail*   **Elaboration**

Football has to be the best sport ever created. <u>It has the greatest action and the coolest plays. Who could forget the cheerleaders?</u> Football is awesome for many reasons.

The first thing <u>I enjoy about football is the action.</u> *What other sport has running, tackling and such exciting throwing? During a football game you can't miss a minute, because the action is really non-stop.* **A lot can happen fast in a football game. Once at an NFL game I went to buy a hot dog, and I missed an interception and a touchdown!**

Also, <u>football has some interesting plays.</u> *The punt return is exciting because anything can happen when the ball is in the hands of the fastest player. Sometimes a quarterback will sneak a running play and surprise the other team. The players all run in different patterns and fake out the defense.* **One time, during a playoff game of my favorite team, the game was won in the last seconds because of a sideways throw of the ball. We ended up scoring and got into the Superbowl.**

<u>Finally, I enjoy watching the cheerleaders.</u> *When my team isn't doing well, they cheer me up. Touchdowns bring a really fancy dance by these talented ladies. They really know how to get a crowd pumped.* **During the halftime show they usually do a dance to some of the most popular songs on the radio. Everyone in the stands dances along.**

In conclusion, football is a great sport due to the action, plays and fabulous cheerleaders. What a great way to spend a Sunday afternoon.

Elaboration

The key to good writing is specific detail. In demand-prompt writing, as mandated by state writing assessments, it is sometimes difficult to encourage the development of the kind of detail needed to support ideas well. In these situations students need to be practiced and polished in planning and adding meaningful detail to their writing.

When using a Four Square writing method, instruction in elaboration can be included in the planning stage. As students complete a Four Square:

First	Also
It's easy	**It's fun to eat**

• Roll the meat
   golf balls
• Throw in pot
   huge cauldron-size
• Pour store-bought sauce
   Mama someone or other
	• Twirl on fork
	   looks like a twister
	• Slurp it
	   loud smacking noise
	• Splatter the sauce
	   like an explosion

My favorite meal is spaghetti and meatballs.

Third	So you can see
It's delicious	

• Tomatoes
   red and tangy
• Italian spices
   zippy garlic
• Filling meat
   like a hamburger
	My favorite meal is spaghetti and meatballs because it's easy to make, fun to eat and delicious.

Have them go back into each box and add a "one time" story. Simply add a personal anecdote or creative tidbit that supports the topic. In the "It's easy" box, one might add a short memoir about the time that 20 people were coming for dinner, and the spaghetti and meatballs were ready in no time, and everyone loved them. Adding an idea like this supports the topic, provides personal anecdote and meaningful detail. In the "It's fun to eat" box a supportive elaboration is likely to include a food fight. The "It's delicious" box might add an elaboration about ordering spaghetti and meatballs at my favorite restaurant for my birthday dinner every year.

90

To add in elaboration to the four square graphic organizer, only a few short words about it are necessary. At the bottom of the boxes, plan the elaboration ahead of time, and the drafting of the story will practically write itself.

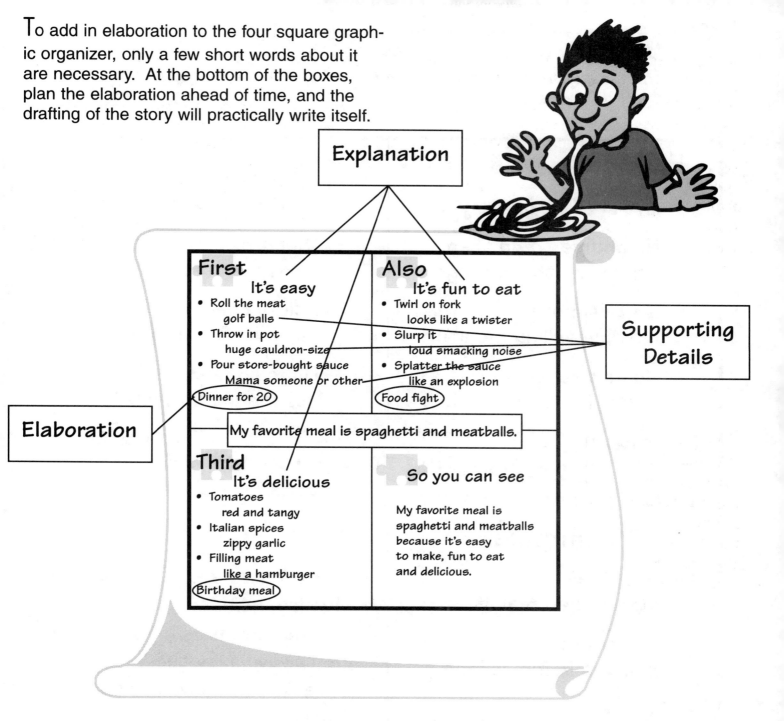

Explanation

Supporting Details

Elaboration

First
It's easy
• Roll the meat
   golf balls
• Throw in pot
   huge cauldron-size
• Pour store-bought sauce
   Mama someone or other
(Dinner for 20)

Also
It's fun to eat
• Twirl on fork
   looks like a twister
• Slurp it
   loud smacking noise
• Splatter the sauce
   like an explosion
(Food fight)

My favorite meal is spaghetti and meatballs.

Third
It's delicious
• Tomatoes
   red and tangy
• Italian spices
   zippy garlic
• Filling meat
   like a hamburger
(Birthday meal)

So you can see

My favorite meal is
spaghetti and meatballs
because it's easy
to make, fun to eat
and delicious.

Page 87 has an example of this elaborated story.

In the Four Square method, have students add elaboration to the formula. An essay with all three levels of detail could be well designed using a 4☐ + 3 + C + V + <u>E</u>. When adding elaboration (+ <u>E</u>) to the Four Square formula, think of one anecdote, example, or "one time story" per box. This will help to develop richness of detail. Only a few key words are needed in the four square. The story can be written out in the essay! The following pages contain completed Four Squares and the essays they make. Have your students complete the same highlighting exercise <u>on the Four Square</u> and the essay. Then have them try the exercise where they fill out a Four Square from a completed essay. This "working backwards" exercise really helps them see it all in action. It is a reading comprehension skill that helps students look at things with a "writer's eye."

Name _____

Using three crayons or markers, highlight the explanation in green, the supporting detail in yellow and the elaboration in pink. Notice the patterns in the Four Square.

First

It's a getaway

- **No chores to do there**
  take out the garbage

- **No telephone**
  people selling me stuff

- **No interruptions**
  little brother

(Carpenter)

Also

The snacks

- **Popcorn**
  extra butter

- **Sticky candies**
  in your teeth for days

- **Huge soda pop**
  costs about $6.00

(Birthday)

I enjoy going to the movies.

Mostly

The movies!

- **Big Screen**
  bigger than real life

- **New movies**
  months before videos

- **Previews**
  what's coming soon

(Jaws)

So you can see,
I enjoy going to the
movies because I like a
getaway, enjoy the
snacks and I love seeing
movies.

Find the three levels of support in the following essay, just as you did in the Four Square. Color the explanation green, the supporting detail yellow and the elaboration red.

When I want a night out, my favorite place to go is to the movies. I think it's a great getaway. The snacks are huge and delicious. And I just love seeing those movies.

First, I just enjoy the getaway. At a theater I know that I have no chores to do. I can't take out the garbage there! The telephone won't ring with someone annoying me to buy something. Interruptions are few when I leave my little brother home! When there was a carpenter working on my house, we kept getting underfoot, so my mom took us to the movies. We loved the getaway, and the work could get done at home without us nosy-bodies.

The snacks are also great at the movies. Everybody knows that there is no better popcorn than movie theater popcorn. Last year, for my birthday sleepover party, my mom stopped at the local movie theater to get us real popcorn for the party. It was a great hit. The sticky candies, that are in your teeth for days, are delicious. I like the huge, sweet and cold soda, even though it costs about $6.00.

Mostly, I like going to the movies for the movies themselves. Watching on a big screen

lets you see the action larger than in real life. My mom said that she saw *Jaws* on the big screen when she was a kid, and it scared her half to death! It just doesn't have the same effect on video. Besides, I can see the new movies months before they come out on tape or DVD. Those previews before the movie let us know what movies to look forward to in the future.

Clearly, going to the movies is something I enjoy. The getaway, the snacks and mostly the movies themselves make going to the movies so much fun for me.

Answer Key

First

It's a getaway

- No chores to do there
  take out the garbage

- No telephone
  people selling me stuff

- No interruptions
  little brother

(Carpenter)

Also

The snacks

- Popcorn
  extra butter

- Sticky candies
  in your teeth for days

- Huge soda pop
  costs about $6.00

(Birthday)

I enjoy going to the movies.

Mostly

The movies!

- Big Screen
  bigger than real life

- New movies
  months before videos

- Previews
  what's coming soon

(Jaws)

So you can see,
I enjoy going to the
movies because I like a
getaway, enjoy the
snacks, and I love seeing
movies.

Answer Key

Some of these answers are subject to discussion, and discussion is good!

<u>Explanation</u>   *Supporting Detail*   **Elaboration**

When I want a night out, my favorite place to go is to the movies. <u>I think it's a great getaway. The snacks are huge and delicious. And I just love seeing those movies.</u>

First, I just <u>enjoy the getaway.</u> *At a theater I know that I have no chores to do. I can't take out the garbage there! The telephone won't ring with someone annoying me to buy something. Interruptions are few when I leave my little brother home!* **When there was a carpenter working on my house, we kept getting underfoot, so my mom took us to the movies. We loved the getaway, and the work could get done at home without us nosy-bodies.**

<u>The snacks are also great at the movies.</u> *Everybody knows that there is no better popcorn than movie theater popcorn.* **Last year, for my birthday sleepover party, my mom stopped at the local movie theater to get us real popcorn for the party. It was a great hit.** *The sticky candies, that are in your teeth for days, are delicious. I like the huge, sweet and cold soda, even though it costs about $6.00.*

Mostly, <u>I like going to the movies for the movies themselves.</u> *Watching on a big screen lets you see the action larger than in real life.* **My mom said that she saw *Jaws* on the big screen when she was a kid, and it scared her half to death! It just doesn't have the same effect on video.** *Besides, I can see the new movies months before they come out on tape or DVD. Those previews before the movie let us know what movies to look forward to in the future.*

Clearly, going to the movies is something I enjoy. The getaway, the snacks and mostly the movies themselves make going to the movies so much fun for me.

Name _____

Using three crayons or markers, highlight the explanation in green, the supporting detail in yellow and the elaboration in pink. Notice the patterns in the Four Square.

One reason
Great weather

- Warm and pleasant
  no jackets to wear

- Stay outside
  play with friends

- Bright sunshine
  get a tan

(Long day out)

In addition
Sports

- Swimming
  pool, lake, beach

- Baseball
  America's pastime

- Skating
  around the neighborhood

(Neighborhood)

| Summer is my favorite season. |

As well
Vacation

- Travel
  visit relatives

- Sleep in
  don't feel tired

- Relax
  no homework

(Camp trip)

Hence, summer is my favorite season because I enjoy the weather, the summer sports, and summer vacation.

Name _____

Find the three levels of support in the following essay, just as you did in the Four Square. Color the explanation green, the supporting detail yellow and the elaboration red.

Summer is my favorite season for several reasons. I enjoy the weather in summer. It is a great time for all the sports that I am crazy about. Vacationing in summer makes the year complete. There are many reasons why summer is probably any kid's favorite season.

One reason is the great weather. It is warm and pleasant outside, and there is no need to mess around with a coat or a jacket. In the summer I can play outside with my friends. In fact, I usually go out right after breakfast and don't come in until lunch. In summer I'm outside about 12 hours per day! The bright sunshine also gives my skin a healthy glow and a tan.

In addition to the weather, summer has great sports. Swimming is great, whether at the pool, lake or beach. Summer is the time for baseball, a sport I love, and America's pastime. Once my friends and I had a neighborhood game of baseball going on that lasted 19 innings! In the neighborhood I sometimes like to skate around all day.

Summer is great because of vacations as well. We always travel in summer and visit family that lives far away. Every summer my family and I pack up for a big camping trip. We camp by a lake up in the mountains and play all day. Because we are on vacation, my mom lets me sleep in, and I don't feel so tired. It's nice to relax and get a break from homework for a little while.

Hence, summer is my favorite season because I enjoy the weather, the summer sports and summer vacation. I sometimes wish it could be summer all year!

Answer Key

<u>Explanation</u>   Supporting Detail   Elaboration

One reason
<u>Great weather</u>

- Warm and pleasant
  no jackets to wear

- Stay outside
  play with friends

- Bright sunshine
  get a tan

(Long day out)

In addition
<u>Sports</u>

- Swimming
  pool, lake, beach

- Baseball
  America's pastime

- Skating
  around the neighborhood

(Neighborhood)

Summer is my favorite season.

As well
<u>Vacation</u>

- Travel
  visit relatives

- Sleep in
  don't feel tired

- relax
  no homework

(Camp trip)

Hence, summer is my favorite season because I enjoy the weather, the summer sports, and summer vacation.

Answer Key

Some of these answers are subject to discussion, and discussion is good!

<u>Explanation</u>   *Supporting Detail*   **Elaboration**

Summer is my favorite season for several reasons. <u>I enjoy the weather in summer. It is a great time for all the sports that I am crazy about. Vacationing in summer makes the year complete.</u> There are many reasons why summer is probably any kid's favorite season.

One reason is <u>the great weather.</u> **It is warm and pleasant outside, and there is no need to mess around with a coat or a jacket. In the summer I can play outside with my friends. In fact, I usually go out right after breakfast and don't come in until lunch.** *In summer I'm outside about 12 hours per day! The bright sunshine also gives my skin a healthy glow and a tan.*

In addition to the weather, summer <u>has great sports.</u> *Swimming is great, whether at the pool, lake or beach. Summer is the time for baseball, a sport I love, and America's pastime.* **Once my friends and I had a neighborhood game of baseball going on that lasted 19 innings!** *In the neighborhood I sometimes like to skate around all day.*

Summer is great <u>because of vacations as well.</u> *We always travel in summer and visit family that lives far away. Every summer my family and I pack up for a big camping trip.* **We camp by a lake up in the mountains and play all day.** *Because we are on vacation, my mom lets me sleep in, and I don't feel so tired. It's nice to relax and get a break from homework for a little while.*

Hence, summer is my favorite season because I enjoy the weather, the summer sports and summer vacation. I sometimes wish it could be summer all year!

Read the following essay and look for the three levels of support.

Computers are a really great invention. They make getting information so easy. I use my computer to keep in touch and shop. I don't know where I'd be without it.

To begin with, computers are a fabulous way to get information. Research can be done at your fingertips. When I had to do a research paper for my class, I was able to get the magazine articles and encyclopedia entries on-line, at home, in my pajamas! On-line there is government information in full-text and product recalls on items for safety.

In addition, my computer helps me to keep in touch. E-mail works so much faster than regular mail. Instant messaging allows me to chat with friends far away. It isn't all playing around, either. I was doing homework last week when I just couldn't find the answers to my literature questions. Well, some of my friends were on-line, so I asked them. We completed the assignment that way! Keeping in touch with pen pals and sending pictures and videos has never been easier.

Finally, shopping on-line is a blast. It is easy to buy things with just one click. I can compare prices for thousands of companies without leaving home. My mom gets e-mail updates from her favorite stores, telling her about bargains and sales. She buys a lot on-line, but especially our airplane tickets. She once got us tickets to DisneyWorld that only cost $50.

So you can see, computers are a great invention because they help us get information, keep in touch and shop. I can't imagine life without my computer.

Read the essay on the previous page. Look for the three levels of support as you read.
Now complete this Four Square based on the information in the essay.

Answer Key

To begin with
Information

- Research
  at your fingertips

- Government information
  full text

- Product recalls
  safety

(Research paper)

In addition
Keep in touch

- E-mail
  faster than regular mail

- Instant messages
  chat with friends far away

- Send pictures
  even video

(Homework help)

Computers are a great invention.

Finally
Shopping

- Easy
  click

- Compare prices
  thousands of companies

- E-mail updates
  sales and bargains

(Airline tickets)

So you can see,
computers are a great
invention because they
help us get information,
keep in touch and shop.

Improving Narrative Writing

While narrative writing can take many forms and serve many functions, using the Four Square organizer can help students get started when facing the blank paper. It also is very useful on occasions when students must produce a narrative on demand, like in an assessment situation.

In the first Four Square series, narrative writing is addressed. It is contrasted from expository or persuasive writing because it is driven by actions and emotions. While it is a very different style of writing, it is still important to provide systematic and step-by-step instruction in the planning and improvement of narrative writing.

The development of detail in the narrative can be difficult for students. Many tend to explain the story, when we really wish they could tell the story through the eyes and ears of the writer or narrator. Some modifications have been made to the Four Square form to help students plan and accomplish this. For the "plus three" stage of planning, writers are asked to add **one** detail about what they see, **one** about what they hear and **one** about the character's feelings. In this way the detail is developed meaningfully. The improved planner follows, along with a completed one and some practice pages. In addition, several strategies are included for revising and improving narrative drafts.

Four Square Books

Four Square Writing Method Series

TLC10188   Grades 1-3
TLC10189   Grades 4-6
TLC10190   Grades 7-9

Four Square: The Total Writing Classroom Series

TLC10333   Grades 1-4
TLC10334   Grades 5-9

Written by Judith S. and Evan Jay Gould

4□ + 3 + C + V Narrative

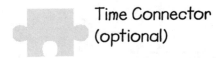

 Time Connector
(optional)

 Time Connector
(optional)

Action 1 (Cause)
Usually the prompt; the whole reason that we are telling the story. Must include a verb!

 **See** | Vivid Sensory detail or elaboration

 **Hear** | Vivid Sensory detail or elaboration

Feel | Vivid Sensory detail or elaboration

Action 2 (Effect)
The next action (verb) that happens!

 See | Vivid Sensory detail or elaboration

 Hear | Vivid Sensory detail or elaboration

Feel | Vivid Sensory detail or elaboration

Setting/Characters before the action

Who? _____

What? _____

Where? _____

When? _____

 Time Connector
(optional)

 Time Connector
(optional)

Action 3 (Consequence)
Yet another action (verb) happens.

 **See** | Vivid Sensory detail or elaboration

 **Hear** | Vivid Sensory detail or elaboration

Feel | Vivid Sensory detail or elaboration

Solution
How it all ends . . .

104

4□ + 3 + C + V Narrative

 Suddenly

 After careful thought

Mom was gone

Decided to tell a saleslady

 See — Nothing in the spot where she was standing.

 Hear — Other kids talking to their moms around the store.

 Feel — Scared and alone

 See — A lady in a pretty dress with a name tag on.

 Hear — "I'm only five years old, and my mommy is lost."

 **Feel** — Embarrassed when she laughed and took my hand.

Setting/Characters before the action

Who? <u>My mom and I</u>

What? <u>Buying school clothes</u>

Where? <u>A massive mall</u>

When? <u>When I was five years old</u>

So

In a few minutes

Brought me to an office

Solution

 **See** — Lots of salespeople and a big speaker system

 **Hear** — Asked my name, announced it for the whole store to hear

 Feel — Pretty important to have my name said out loud in the massive store

- Mom came.
- Thanked saleslady.
- Said she was proud of me, I handled it well.
- We went for ice cream.

Sample Narrative Essay

Using the Revised 4□ + 3 + C + V Plus Editing

Use three markers (green, yellow and red) to highlight the details included in this story. Use green to show what the character sees, yellow for what is heard and red to show how the character feels.

Sometimes a bad thing happens, but it has a good outcome. That's the way it was when I was five years old. My mom and I were shopping in the mall for my kindergarten clothes. It was a massive store. That was part of the problem.

Things were fine until I turned around and found that my mom had suddenly disappeared. The spot where she was standing and looking at shirts was now empty. She was nowhere to be found! Instead of her voice, I heard the other voices of happy kids talking to their moms. Their moms weren't lost! I suddenly felt very scared and alone.

After some careful thought I decided I should tell a saleslady. I looked behind the counter and saw a lady in a pretty dress. She wore a name tag that said *Betsy*. Thinking that she must be in charge, I told her, "I'm only five years old and my mommy is lost." I didn't know why she laughed at me, but she took my hand and told me it would be okay. I was really embarrassed.

So she brought me to a large office. It was filled with salespeople from the store. There was a speaker system with a microphone there, too. Another lady, sitting behind the speaker system, asked me my name. Then she said it out loud, into the microphone, for the whole store to hear. Suddenly, I didn't feel scared, but proud instead. I was in this important office, and the whole, entire store just found out about it!

In just a few minutes my mom found her way to that important office too, but she didn't look proud. She said that she was worried about me. After thanking the saleslady, she told me how proud she was, and that I had done the right thing. We left that store and went to get some ice cream. So a bad thing turned out pretty well for me that day.

Answer Key

Some of these answers are subject to discussion, and discussion is good!

<u>Green</u>   Yellow   **Red**

Sometimes a bad thing happens, but it has a good outcome. That's the way it was when I was five years old. My mom and I were shopping in the mall for my kindergarten clothes. It was a massive store. That was part of the problem.

Things were fine until I turned around and found that my mom had suddenly disappeared. <u>The spot where she was standing and looking at shirts was now empty. She was nowhere to be found!</u> *Instead of her voice, I heard the other voices of happy kids talking to their moms.* **Their moms weren't lost! I suddenly felt very scared and alone.**

After some careful thought I decided I should tell a saleslady. <u>I looked behind the counter and saw a lady in a pretty dress. She wore a name tag that said Betsy.</u> *Thinking that she must be in charge, I told her, "I'm only five years old and my mommy is lost."* I didn't know why she laughed at me, but she took my hand and told me it would be okay. I was really embarrassed.

So she brought me to a large office. <u>It was filled with salespeople from the store. There was a speaker system with a microphone there, too.</u> *Another lady, sitting behind the speaker system, asked me my name. Then she said it out loud, into the microphone, for the whole store to hear.* **Suddenly, I didn't feel scared, but proud instead. I was in this important office, and the whole, entire store just found out about it!**

In just a few minutes my mom found her way to that important office too, but she didn't look proud. She said that she was worried about me. After thanking the saleslady, she told me how proud she was, and that I had done the right thing. We left that store and went to get some ice cream. So a bad thing turned out pretty well for me that day.

Editing the Narrative

1. Hit the "pause" button.

Imagine the story as running on a video-tape. During an interesting moment you press "pause." In this way you stop in the story to capture a moment of description. Action halts and the writer focuses on one object, character or setting. This should be four to five sentences in length. There should be no action during the pause. Pauses should be used judiciously.

Teaching Tip
Pauses are like family vacation photos. Think about a trip to the Pyramids. What pictures would other people want to see? Brushing your teeth at the Motel 6 or the tomb of Tutankhamen?

2. Show a feeling, don't just tell it.

A stop in the story to capture a character's feelings. Action halts and the writer focuses on the body language and facial expressions of one character or group of characters. Showing a feeling should be four to five sentences in length. It should describe the physical appearance of the character without making a general statement of the feeling.

Teaching Tip
This is a situation of "Show, Don't Tell." (See pages 76-77.) Play-act different feelings and have the students guess the emotion. Chart the physical attributes for common feelings. Readers like to have help getting the mental/visual picture of the character at emotional key points in the story.

3. Use the 1, 2, 3 punch to build suspense.

This is a method of building suspense in narrative writing. It slows down the discovery of a plot turn, creating reader interest. The 1, 2, 3 punch gives a hint, and then describes the characters reaction through thought or action. Then there is a greater hint, and a larger reaction. Finally, with the third hint, the character makes the plot-turning discovery.

Teaching Tip
Play-act and practice in groups. Give each group a "discovery card" (See reproducibles on pages 111-112.), and they can practice writing the 1, 2, 3 punch to build suspense prior to the discovery. Encourage the inclusion of characters' thoughts. They really bring readers into the story.

4. Don't speed through the best part! Hit "slow motion"!

Slow motion should be used at the climax of the story, usually the point at which the problem is solved. This should be the pinnacle of reader interest and excitement. The slow motion is the film roll pulled out of the camera and described frame by frame. Break down general actions and add character feelings and dialogue.

Teaching Tip
*Have students practice using some actions that go very quickly (falling on a banana peel). Challenge students to write that action in the **most** sentences possible, including frame-by-frame action, character thought and feelings.*

5. Sometimes you need to plan before you plan.

Before you get started you should have an idea of the destination. The Story Plan helps to focus stories. The Story Plan is a simple, cloze activity that can solve a lot of the story wandering by student writers. You may ask students to complete a story plan even before making a four square.

This is a story about _____.
(character)

The problem is that _____

_____

_____.

The problem is solved when _____

_____

_____.

On the following page, the narrative is rewritten with all these elements included.

Sample Narrative Essay

Using the Revised 4□ + 3 + C + V Plus Editing

Sometimes a bad thing happens, but it has a good outcome. That's the way it was when I was five years old. My mom and I were shopping in the mall for my kindergarten clothes. It was a massive store. That was part of the problem.

1, 2, 3 Punch →

Things were fine until I turned around. I knew that my mom was standing beside me. Was she hiding, I thought. No, she wouldn't trick me. Maybe she had a great surprise for me. But she wouldn't leave me alone in this big place. No, I realized, my mom had suddenly disappeared. I got pale and started trembling. My bottom lip began to quiver on its own and I felt sweat on my brow. I suddenly felt like I had to go to the bathroom. The spot where she was standing and looking at shirts was now empty. She was nowhere to be found! Instead of her voice, I heard the other voices of happy kids talking to their moms. Their moms weren't lost! I suddenly felt very scared and alone.

← **Showing Feeling**

After some careful thought I decided I should tell a saleslady. I looked behind the counter and saw a lady in a pretty dress. She wore a name tag that said *Betsy*. Thinking that she must be in charge, I told her, "I'm only five years old and my mommy is lost." I didn't know why she laughed at me, but she took my hand and told me it would be okay. I was really embarrassed.

So she brought me to a large office. It was filled with salespeople from the store. There were tan leather couches surrounding the room. I could smell the coffee brewing in the coffeepot in the corner. The room had a loud buzz of people talking. I saw posters on the wall and a portrait of a very important man. I thought that he must be the owner of the store. There was a speaker system with a microphone there, too. Another lady, sitting behind the speaker system, asked me my name. Then she said it out loud, into the microphone, for the whole store to hear. Suddenly, I didn't feel scared, but proud instead. I was in this important office, and the whole, entire store just found out about it!

← **Pause Button**

Slow Motion →

In just a few minutes I saw a familiar face. My mom was entering the room. She was trembling slightly, and her hair, that was usually perfect, looked kind of messy. As she ran towards me her arms were outstretched. She had a tear in her left eye. "What's wrong, Mom?" I asked. She didn't answer right away. She hugged me. Then she thanked the saleslady and told me that she was proud of me, and I had done the right thing. We left that store and went to get some ice cream. So a bad thing turned out pretty well for me that day.

Discovery Card Reproducibles

Practice your 1, 2, 3 punch on
these scenarios or make up your own!

Jane has been baking cookies all morning for her party tonight. When she leaves the kitchen to answer the phone Goldie, the family's large, hungry, cookie-loving dog, enters. Jane returns.

_____
_____
_____
_____
_____
_____
_____
_____

Sam is awakened in the middle of the night by a soft, green light coming from inside his closet. He gets out of bed and walks over to the closet door.

_____
_____
_____
_____
_____
_____
_____
_____

"Every time I open my mouth to take a little bite of food," complained Olivia the Oyster, "another annoying grain of sand finds its way in here."

_____
_____
_____
_____
_____
_____
_____

Discovery Card Reproducibles

Make up your own!